Good Fast Family Food

hamlyn

Good Fast Family Food

Joanna Farrow

First published in Great Britain in 2001 by Hamlyn
an imprint of Octopus Publishing Group Limited
2-4 Heron Quays
London E14 4JP

Copyright © 2001 Octopus Publishing Limited

ISBN 0600 60321 0

British Library Cataloguing-in-Publication Data
A catalogue record for this book is available from the British Library

Printed in China

10 9 8 7 6 5 4 3 2 1

NOTES

All recipes serve 4 unless otherwise stated.

Standard level spoon measures are used in all recipes
1 tablespoon = one 15 ml spoon
1 teaspoon = one 5 ml spoon

Both metric and imperial measurements are given for the recipes. Use one set of measures only, not a mixture of both.

Ovens should be preheated to the specified temperature. If using a fan-assisted oven, follow the manufacturer's instructions for adjusting the time and temperature. Grills should also be preheated.

Free-range medium eggs should be used unless otherwise specified.

Use full-fat milk unless otherwise suggested.

Pepper should be freshly ground unless otherwise specified.

Fresh herbs should be used unless otherwise stated. If unobtainable, use dried herbs as an alternative but halve the quantities stated.

A few recipes include nuts and nut derivatives. Anyone with a known nut allergy must avoid these. Children under the age of 3 with a family history of nut allergy, asthma, eczema or any other type of allergy are also advised to avoid eating dishes that contain nuts.

Contents

Introduction

In recent years, nutritional studies have highlighted the links between diet and health. The importance of a good healthy diet is now widely recognized and the phrase 'you are what you eat' has never been so clearly understood.

From a baby's first milk, through childhood and adolescence, a good diet paves the way to a healthy adult life. And it doesn't stop there. As adults, we can benefit from increased energy and vitality, fewer ailments and the potential of an extended life-span in good health if we maintain a healthy, balanced diet. Even our ability to concentrate, retain information, think clearly and sleep well is governed in part by our diet. Conversely, there are now indications that living on TV dinners, takeaways, highly refined foods and those which have been chemically treated can be detrimental to health.

Healthy eating habits and the practice of eating together as a family is fast taking second place to work pressures and the complex commitments of family life. The week evolves at such a hectic pace that planning a varied menu, let alone shopping for it, is a low priority. It's all too easy to resort to ready-made freezer meals or takeaways.

This innovative cookbook makes it easy to provide healthy meals for all, within the constraints of a busy family lifestyle. It acknowledges that meals need to be easy to assemble – often on demand – and not overburdened with countless ingredients. There are fresh new ideas for all occasions, as well as quick and easy healthy updates on old favourites. Even the increasing likelihood of at least one vegetarian in the family is catered for.

So that you can provide your family with a balanced diet, it's useful to have a basic understanding of nutrients, their functions and how they are best obtained in the family diet. Every cell in the body is made up from the nutrients in the food we eat – a combination of water, protein, fat, vitamins and minerals – each nutrient playing an absolutely vital role.

WATER

Water accounts for about two thirds of the body weight and is essential to life. Water aids the digestion of food and absorption of nutrients, and helps to eliminate waste. While a healthy adult can survive without food for up to a few weeks, the body cannot do without water for more than a couple of days. Bearing in mind that the body excretes 1.5 litres (2½ pints) a day, we need to replace it by drinking about 2 litres (3½ pints) a day. This can be taken as neat water, used to dilute fruit juice, or in herbal teas. Alcohol, tea and coffee do not count as valuable liquids; in fact they are diuretics, which increase the amount of water excreted and reduce the absorption of valuable nutrients into the body.

Most tap water is sufficiently clean to drink. It's checked periodically for chemical traces as well as levels of chlorine, fluoride and lime. Even so, many people prefer to filter tap water to remove chemical residues, or buy bottled water.

PRACTICAL TIPS
• Drink plenty of water every day and encourage your children to do so too. Always put a jug of water on the dining table.
• Instead of fizzy drinks, give children fruit juices topped up with sparkling water.
• Accompany drinks of tea and coffee with a glass of water to dilute their adverse effects on the digestive system.

PROTEIN

Protein is vital for the growth and repair of tissue in the muscles, bones, skin, nails and hair. It's also essential for the production of hormones, enzymes and antibodies, for brain functioning and transporting substances around the body. A lack of protein in the diet will retard growth, though this is rare. Excess protein cannot be stored and is broken down into glucose and by-products, which can put a strain on the liver, kidneys and heart.

Protein is made up of differing combinations of 20 amino acids, many of which the human body can make for itself. There are however eight essential amino acids which must be obtained from the diet. Meat and dairy produce – the animal proteins – contain all the essential amino acids, but also contain a high percentage of undesirable saturated fats.

Vegetable or plant proteins come from a variety of sources, including cereals, brown rice, beans, pulses, nuts, vegetables, fruits, tofu and quorn. These foods are also high in other valuable nutrients and are often considered worthier than animal protein foods. With the exception of soya, proteins from plant sources are lacking in one or more of the essential amino acids. However by eating a variety of these foods – which tends to happen naturally – the mix of proteins will provide all the essential amino acids. So, contrary to traditional thinking, men, women and children can get all the required proteins from vegetable sources, provided their diet is varied and fairly rich in unrefined foods.

PRACTICAL TIPS

• Try to restrict big meat eaters to just two or three major meat meals a week so that the rest of the protein comes from largely vegetable sources – such as pasta, rice, lentil or beans.
• As two thirds of any meal should be carbohydrate-based, keep meat portions relatively small in relation to potatoes, rice etc, and serve a variety of nutrient-rich vegetables.
• Serve high protein vegetables – like broccoli, runner beans, broad beans and peas – regularly as an accompaniment.
• Don't force faddy eaters to eat meat. If necessary remove the meat from their portion and compensate by giving them extra vegetables and carbohydrate, such as pasta, potato or rice.

FATS

Fats provide us with a concentrated source of energy, important fat-soluble vitamins and essential fatty acids, which are needed for a variety of functions, including the correct functioning of the brain and nervous system. Only a relatively small amount of fat is needed, most of us eat too much. A diet that is high in fat can lead to health problems, such as obesity and heart disease. All fats are composed of fatty acids. They're found in meat, fish, dairy produce, vegetable oils, nuts and seeds. Fats can be either 'saturated' or 'unsaturated'.

Saturated fatty acids are the 'hard' fats found in meat and dairy produce. A high intake of these can raise blood cholesterol levels, clog up the arteries and lead to obesity. Saturated fats are not strictly essential in the diet.

Unsaturated fatty acids fall into two groups: monounsaturates and polyunsaturates. Monounsaturated fats are present in olive oil and avocados, and again are not fundamental in the diet. Nuts, seeds, oily fish and vegetable oils are the main sources of polyunsaturates, which are essential in the diet.

We often read on packaging labels 'rich in omega-6' (linoleic acid), or 'rich in omega-3' (linolenic acid). These vital polyunsaturated fatty acids promote a healthy brain, nervous system, immune system, heart and skin. Like many nutrients they are easily destroyed by heat and exposure to oxygen, so having a regular supply is essential.

'Hydrogenated' fats on the other hand should be avoided. These are usually vegetable oils that have been chemically treated to solidify them to make margarine. They are as bad for you, if not worse, than saturated fats.

PRACTICAL TIPS

• To benefit from 'good fats' use olive, sunflower, nut, sesame or pumpkin seed oil for frying in preference to animal fats.
• Try to serve a portion of oily fish such as mackerel, herrings, salmon, tuna or sardines once or twice a week.
• Avoid fatty cuts of meat and trim off visible fat before cooking.
• Sprinkle a tablespoonful of sesame, sunflower or pumpkin seeds over muesli, fruit, yogurt and salads.
• Opt for lower fat cake and biscuit recipes. Saturated fats can often be reduced, substituted with olive oil or omitted altogether.

CARBOHYDRATES

These are the body's main fuel supply and can be either 'fast release' or 'slow release'. Fast-release or simple carbohydrates are found mainly in sugar, sweets, fizzy drinks and other highly refined foods. The sugar from these is quickly absorbed and released into the bloodstream, giving a sudden burst of energy, soon followed by a slump as blood sugar levels fall. This creates a craving for another sweet food. As a result the body suffers fluctuating energy levels, resulting in lethargy and mood swings. A diet that is high in refined sugar often leads to other health problems too, especially tooth decay and sometimes obesity and heart disease. Because fast-release carbohydrates simply provide energy and no other nutrients, we should try to keep them to a minimum.

Slow-release or complex carbohydrates are found mainly in grains and grain products including bread, pasta and rice; pulses and nuts; starchy vegetables such as potatoes; and fruits – especially bananas. Not only do these foods provide a slow, sustained release of energy; they are also high in other nutrients such as fibre, vitamins and minerals. We should aim for these slow-release carbohydrates to make up over half our food.

PRACTICAL TIPS

• Include plenty of grains and pulses in the family's diet, such as grainy, wholemeal or rye bread; porridge oats and oatmeal; cornmeal and sweetcorn; beans, lentils, rice and potatoes.
• Steer children away from sugary breakfast cereals. Instead, encourage them to eat sugar-free oat, corn and wheat based cereals, sprinkled with dried sultanas, raisins or apricots.
• Encourage the family to snack on fruit. A bowl of bite-sized strawberries, grapes, cherries, or cut up fruit, is tempting.
• If possible use brown flour and rice in preference to white, as some nutrients are lost during the refining process. A mixture of brown and white flour is often more successful in baking.

VITAMINS

These are not required in large quantities, but they are vital for activating almost all the body processes. Each vitamin has one or more specific functions. Working with other nutrients they provide energy, build tissue, boost the immune system, promote healthy skin and aid the brain and nervous system. A varied diet that includes plenty of fresh food will provide all the vitamins required. Fast foods and highly refined foods are often lacking in vitamins. The fat-soluble vitamins – A, D, E and K – can be stored by the body, but the water-soluble vitamins – C and B group vitamins – cannot, so a daily intake of these is needed.

Vitamins A, C and E are the main antioxidant vitamins. They are now believed to have anti-ageing properties, in addition to helping protect the body from some forms of cancer, heart disease and other fatal illnesses.

Vitamin A comes in the form of retinol, from animal sources, and beta-carotene – a powerful antioxidant found in red, yellow and orange fruits as well as vegetables.

Vitamin B encompasses a large group of different vitamins, including thiamin (B1), riboflavin (B2), niacin, and folate or folic acid. They are mainly involved in the release of energy, although each B vitamin has several specific tasks. Folate, for example, is vital for reproduction and the production of red blood cells.

Vitamin C is the infection-fighting vitamin. It boosts the immune system, helping to ward off colds and other infections; it also helps wounds to heal. It is also vital for healthy skin, bones and teeth. Rich sources are peppers, watercress, citrus fruits, strawberries, tomatoes, broccoli, cabbage and kiwi fruit.

Vitamin D is needed for strong bones and teeth. Oily fish, eggs, milk and some vegetables are good sources. Vitamin D is also synthesized in the body by the action of sunlight on the skin.

Vitamins are destroyed by oxidation, especially on exposure to heat or light, and during storage, preparation and cooking; Vitamin C is particularly susceptible. After picking, storing and cooking, fruits and vegetables can suffer huge losses.

PRACTICAL TIPS

• Aim to get everyone to eat at least the recommended five portions of different vegetables and fruit every day.
• Buy absolutely fresh fruit and vegetables from a good supplier and make the most of fresh seasonal produce.
• Use fresh in preference to frozen or canned produce. Frozen vegetables, however, make a good substitute if fresh produce looks rather jaded. Frozen peas, sweetcorn and broad beans are particularly useful freezer standbys.
• Steam vegetables in preference to boiling. If you do boil them, keep cooking time to a minimum and keep the cooking water as a base for making soups, stews and gravies.

MINERALS

Like vitamins, minerals are essential for almost every bodily function. The 'macro' or major minerals are calcium, iron, magnesium, phosphorus, potassium and sodium. The minor minerals – or trace elements – are required in smaller amounts, but are nonetheless vital. Deficiency of most minerals is rare, but it is important to ensure that the diet provides enough calcium and iron, in particular. Calcium is needed for strong bones and teeth – milk, dairy products, eggs, canned sardines and salmon (eaten with bones), and dark green leafy vegetables are the best sources. Iron is vital for the production of haemoglobin, the pigment that transports oxygen in the blood. Red meat, especially liver, shellfish, dark green leafy vegetables, wholemeal bread, dried fruit, pulses and egg yolk are good sources.

PRACTICAL TIPS

• Serve mineral-rich foods every day. Good sources of minerals include broccoli, dark green leafy vegetables, runner beans, broad beans, peas, root vegetables, lentils, whole grains and dried beans.

• Shellfish, red meat, eggs, milk and cheese are rich in different minerals, though vegetarians and vegans can obtain sufficient minerals if they have a varied diet.
• Drinking good quality mineral water keeps mineral levels up and helps to clear toxins from the body.

FIBRE

Fibre, an indigestible form of plant carbohydrate, is essential to the body as it absorbs water in the digestive tract and enables food to pass through easily. A lack of fibre in the diet can cause constipation and lead to more serious diseases of the bowel and digestive tract. Anyone on a diet based largely on highly refined foods, meat, eggs and dairy produce is most at risk.

Whole grains, vegetables, fruit, nuts, seeds, rice, beans and pulses are all rich sources of fibre.

PRACTICAL TIPS

• Include raw vegetables in the diet, as they're particularly high in fibre. Cook vegetables lightly to retain as much fibre as possible.
• Add fresh or dried fruit, seeds or nuts to breakfast cereals.
• Provide fibre-rich foods throughout the day. This will happen naturally if the diet is based on unrefined foods.
• Keep sweets and refined snacks to a minimum. These lack fibre and clog up the digestive system. Instead, eat plenty of fruit.

EFFECTS OF COOKING FOOD

Cooking food makes it more digestible, adds flavour and renders some nutrients more readily available, but it can also destroy nutrients. Some cooking methods are healthier than others. Generally, the less food is cooked and the lower the cooking temperature, the better, as more nutrients are retained.

BOILING Cooking vegetables in boiling water can reduce the vitamin B content by as much as 70% and the vitamin C content by up to 50%. The more water used and the longer the food is cooked the greater the nutrient loss. If boiling, keep the vegetable pieces large to reduce surface area, use the minimum of water and cook until the vegetables are soft but retaining texture.

STEAMING This is one of the healthiest ways of cooking vegetables and fish as the steaming process is gentle, and valuable nutrients are not lost in cooking water. If you don't have a steamer, it's worth buying a small, expandable wire-steaming basket that fits snugly into most medium to large saucepans. Steaming vegetables usually takes a little longer than boiling.

FRYING This is the least healthy way to cook. Try to keep fried foods to a minimum, and use vegetable or olive oil in preference to animal fats for frying.

STIR-FRYING This is a safer method than deep or shallow frying as a minimum amount of oil is used. Because the food is cooked quickly, more nutrients are retained.

ROASTING Long roasting in a very hot oven will cause a gradual loss of nutrients. Avoid roasting at too high a temperature as this destroys nutrients, and don't let food burn.

STEWING AND CASSEROLING This method is healthy and easy, as you can use the lengthy cooking time to do other things. Nutrients that seep into the juices are consumed, and more nutrients are retained as they're cooked at a low temperature.

GRILLING AND BARBECUING Grilling is a healthy cooking method, as it is fast and involves the minimum of added fat – a little is needed to keep food moist. Care must be taken, however, to prevent foods charring and burning, which can produce potential carcinogens. This is more likely to be a problem with barbecuing than grilling as it's difficult to control the heat.

Easy Main Meals

Faced with the culinary likes and dislikes of family members, and the task of providing a main meal every day, it's all too tempting to load the freezer with ready meals. The main courses in this chapter – prepared quickly with fresh ingredients – are a healthy, appetizing alternative. Not all cook quickly, but once the preparation is done and the dish is in the oven, you can turn to other things.

PLAICE WITH PEPPERONI

8 skinless plaice fillets

1 small onion or shallot, finely chopped

3 tomatoes, thinly sliced

40 g (1½ oz) pepperoni sausage, thinly sliced

2 tablespoons chopped flat leaf parsley

1 tablespoon olive oil

25 g (1 oz) breadcrumbs

25 g (1 oz) Parmesan cheese, freshly grated

salt and pepper

flat leaf parsley sprigs, to garnish

lime or lemon wedges, to serve

• If plaice isn't available, buy 4 cod or haddock steaks and simply top them with the stuffing mixture, then add the breadcrumbs and cheese.

• To test if fish is cooked through, pierce the thickest part with the tip of a sharp knife. It should flake easily and be white rather than opaque. Cooking times vary according to the size and thickness of fish fillets.

Small amounts of highly seasoned and spiced 'deli' sausages can pep up dishes without detriment to a healthy diet. Most children who like pizza are familiar with pepperoni sausage, so it's a good way to entice faddy eaters to enjoy fish. Buy ready-skinned fish fillets to save time.

Preparation time: 10 minutes **Cooking time:** 20–25 minutes

Lay 4 plaice fillets in a lightly buttered shallow ovenproof dish. Season lightly and scatter with the onion, then the tomato and pepperoni slices. Sprinkle with the parsley and cover with the remaining plaice fillets.

Heat the olive oil in a small frying pan and fry the breadcrumbs until pale golden.

Scatter the breadcrumbs and cheese over the fish. Bake in a preheated oven at 180°C (350°F) Gas Mark 4 for 20–25 minutes until the fish is cooked through.

Serve the fish garnished with parsley and accompanied by lime or lemon wedges, new potatoes and a green salad.

BONUS POINT

• White fish like plaice, cod and haddock are low in fat and very easy to digest. They contain about 15–20% protein and are high in many vitamins and minerals, notably vitamin B12 and iodine.

HERRINGS WITH SPINACH & PARMESAN

Getting children to eat oily fish is usually difficult, especially if they are faced with lots of bones and fish heads! These filleted herrings with their cheesy, bacon and spinach stuffing may well tempt them.

Preparation time: 15 minutes **Cooking time:** About 30 minutes

2 tablespoons olive oil

2 rashers of streaky bacon, rinded and chopped

1 small onion, chopped

25 g (1 oz) breadcrumbs

150 g (5 oz) baby spinach, trimmed

generous pinch of freshly grated nutmeg

25 g (1 oz) Parmesan cheese, freshly grated

8 herring fillets

pepper

• If you've bought a bag of spinach leaves and have some leftover, combine them with other leaves to make a salad accompaniment.
• Because of the saltiness of the bacon you probably won't need to add salt to the stuffing.

Heat 1 tablespoon of the olive oil in a frying pan, add the bacon and fry for 3 minutes. Add the onion and fry for a further 3–4 minutes until it is softened and the bacon is golden. Add the breadcrumbs and fry for 1 minute.

Stir in the spinach, nutmeg and a little pepper and cook until the spinach has wilted. Add the cheese and remove the pan from the heat.

Lay 4 herring fillets, skin-side down, in a shallow ovenproof dish. Spoon the spinach mixture over the fish fillets then cover it with the remaining 4 fillets, placing them skin-side up. Drizzle with the remaining oil and bake in a preheated oven at 180°C (350°F) Gas Mark 4 for about 20–25 minutes until the fish is cooked through. Serve with new potatoes and grilled tomatoes.

BONUS POINTS
• Oily fish, such as herring, are a rich source of omega-3 fatty acids. These are the essential fatty acids that the body cannot make from other sources, so must be obtained from food. They are important for maintaining healthy cell membranes, and help to protect against circulation and heart problems by assisting blood flow.
• Herring is also an excellent source of protein and vitamins A, B12 and D.

FISH BURGERS WITH YOGURT MAYO

Made by simply whizzing the ingredients together in the food processor, these mildly flavoured burgers are a good way of getting fussy eaters to enjoy fresh fish. Serve in wholegrain buns or with jacket potatoes.

Preparation time: 15 minutes **Cooking time:** 6 minutes

500 g (1 lb) skinless cod or haddock fillet
4 spring onions, trimmed and roughly
    chopped
1 egg white
50 g (2 oz) white breadcrumbs
2 tablespoons sunflower or vegetable oil
salt and pepper

To serve:
3 tablespoons Greek yogurt
3 tablespoons mayonnaise
4 grainy buns
salad leaves

• For a substantial meal, serve with a salad and oven-baked jacket chips (see page 26).
• For a milder flavour, use ½ small onion instead of the spring onions.
• These fish burgers can be grilled successfully. Brush both sides with oil and cook on a foil-lined grill rack under a moderate heat for about 5 minutes on each side.
• Flavour the yogurt mayonnaise with finely chopped fresh herbs, such as tarragon, coriander or dill, if you like.

Check over the fish for any bones, then cut into pieces. Put the fish in a food processor or blender with the spring onions and process briefly until the ingredients are finely chopped. Add the egg white, breadcrumbs and a little salt and pepper and process briefly until the ingredients are combined.

Divide the mixture into 4 portions and shape each one into a flat burger. (Wet the palms of your hands before shaping so the mixture doesn't stick).

Heat the oil in a frying pan and fry the burgers for about 3 minutes on each side until golden and firm.

Meanwhile mix together the yogurt, mayonnaise and a little salt and pepper. Split the buns and pile salad leaves on to each base. Put the burgers on top of the salad and add a spoonful of yogurt mayonnaise. Sandwich together with the burger tops and serve.

BONUS POINT
• White fish like cod and haddock are a concentrated source of protein, low in fat and very easy to digest. They are rich in vitamin B12, which is essential for a healthy nervous system.

GLAZED CHICKEN & PEPPERS

This dish couldn't be easier – it's simply baked in the oven, all in one pan!
Serve it with rice or jacket potatoes, and a simple salad or green vegetable.

Preparation time: 15 minutes **Cooking time:** 40 minutes

4 boneless, skinless chicken breasts

1 small onion, thinly sliced

2 red peppers, cored, deseeded and cut
    into chunks

2 orange or yellow peppers, cored,
    deseeded and cut into chunks

2 garlic cloves, crushed

3 tablespoons olive oil

2 courgettes, thickly sliced

salt and pepper

Glaze:

1 tablespoon clear honey

2 teaspoons sweet chilli sauce

2 tablespoons tomato paste

1 tablespoon Worcestershire sauce

1 teaspoon cornflour

2 tablespoons orange juice

salt and pepper

Pat the chicken breasts dry on kitchen paper and cut each one into 6 chunks.
Place them in a large roasting tin or shallow ovenproof dish with the onion
and peppers. Mix the garlic with the oil and salt and pepper, add to the
roasting tin and toss the ingredients together. Bake in a preheated oven at
220°C (425°F) Gas Mark 7 for 15 minutes.

Add the courgettes to the tin and cook for a further 20 minutes until the
chicken is cooked and the vegetables are lightly coloured.

Meanwhile mix together the ingredients for the glaze. Add to the roasting
tin and toss until the ingredients are coated in the glaze. Cook for a further
5 minutes. Serve accompanied by a simple mixed salad, sprinkled with a little
olive oil and balsamic vinegar.

BONUS POINTS

• Cooking chicken portions without the skin considerably reduces fat intake.
Skin is easily removed from breast portions.

• Red peppers contain high levels of vitamin C to boost the immune system,
and beta-carotene – an important antioxidant that helps general health and
offers some protection from the ageing process.

• A jar of sweet chilli sauce is a
useful storecupboard standby –
perfect for zipping up sauces and
dressings in an instant. Use
cautiously until you're familiar with
the product, as brands vary
considerably in 'hotness'.

TURKEY STEAKS WITH PAPRIKA

Cooked off the bone, turkey breast can be rather dry and bland in flavour, but a spicy coating transforms it to delicious effect – especially if you marinate the meat for a while. This is a good recipe to assemble early in the day, ready for quick and easy cooking when it's time to eat.

Preparation time: 15 minutes **Cooking time:** 15–30 minutes

250 g (8 oz) red Camargue or long-grain rice

4 turkey breast steaks

2 tablespoons tomato ketchup

1 tablespoon paprika

finely grated rind and juice of ½ lemon or lime

3 garlic cloves, crushed

2 teaspoons soy sauce

1 tablespoon olive oil

100 g (3½ oz) baby corn, halved, or frozen sweetcorn

4 slices of fresh or canned pineapple, cut into pieces

salt and pepper

small handful of coriander leaves, chopped (optional)

Cook the rice in plenty of lightly salted boiling water until just tender: about 30 minutes for red rice; 10–15 minutes for ordinary long-grain.

Meanwhile, pat the turkey breasts dry on kitchen paper and score on one side several times with a sharp knife.

In a large bowl, mix together the tomato ketchup, paprika, lemon or lime rind and juice, garlic and soy sauce. Add the turkey steaks and turn them to coat in the glaze.

Heat the oil in a frying pan. Add the turkey steaks, scored-side down, and fry for 4–5 minutes on each side until cooked through.

When the rice is just cooked, add the corn and cook for a further 2 minutes. Drain, return to the pan and stir in the pineapple pieces. Transfer to serving plates, top with the turkey steaks and scatter with coriander, if using.

BONUS POINT

• With less than 2% fat, turkey breast meat is one of the leanest meats – ideal for a healthy diet. Typically, in this country, fat provides about 40% of the calorie intake, which is far more than the recommended amount. In the Far East, much less fat is consumed, resulting in lower rates of heart disease and other fat-related diseases.

LAMBS' LIVER JAMAICAN STYLE

This tasty dish of mildly flavoured, tender lambs' liver in a sweet, spicy coating may tempt even those who have an aversion to offal.

Preparation time: 10 minutes **Cooking time:** 5 minutes

1 small red onion, finely chopped
¼ teaspoon dried chilli flakes
½ teaspoon ground allspice
4 teaspoons light muscovado sugar
1 tablespoon white wine vinegar
1 tablespoon chopped thyme
3 tablespoons vegetable or sunflower oil
500 g (1 lb) thinly sliced lamb's liver
4 tablespoons pineapple or apple juice
salt and pepper

• This recipe works equally well with white fish fillets, boneless chicken thighs, or lamb or pork chops. Fry until cooked through, turning once.
• For convenience the liver can be tossed in the spice mixture and left to marinade for several hours until ready to cook.
• Liver should never be eaten rare (when blood is visible on slicing) although it can be served slightly pink. Avoid overcooking as this quickly toughens liver.

In a large bowl, mix together the onion, chilli flakes, allspice, sugar, vinegar, thyme, salt and pepper and 1 tablespoon of the oil. Trim the liver and cut into thick strips. Add to the bowl and toss to coat thoroughly.

Heat the remaining oil in a frying pan, tip the liver mixture into the pan and stir-fry for about 3 minutes until the liver is cooked through. Remove with a slotted spoon and transfer to warmed serving plates.

Add the fruit juice to the pan and heat until bubbling, scraping up the pan juices. Spoon this glaze over the liver. Serve with jacket potatoes or couscous, and a tomato salad.

BONUS POINTS
• Liver is an excellent source of iron, which is essential for the formation of red blood cells, as well as vitamins A, riboflavin and B12. However, women who are pregnant or trying to conceive should avoid liver because the high level of vitamin A can be a contributory factor in birth defects.
• Like other meat, liver is rich in protein and provides a variety of other nutrients, though it is higher in cholesterol.

RATATOUILLE LAMB PIE

Ratatouille and lamb complement each other perfectly – the tangy tomato and pepper flavours balancing the richness of the lamb. Here they are combined and topped with filo pastry to make a sustaining pie. If you're out for the day, assemble the dish in advance, ready to bake on your return.

Preparation time: 20 minutes   **Cooking time:** 50 minutes

500 g (1 lb) lean lamb fillet

3 tablespoons olive oil

1 small aubergine, about 300 g (10 oz), cut into small dice

2 onions, chopped

2 garlic cloves, crushed

400 g (13 oz) can chopped tomatoes

2 tablespoons sun-dried tomato paste

2 red peppers, cored, deseeded and roughly chopped

2 courgettes, sliced

1 tablespoon chopped thyme

3 sheets filo pastry, about 150 g (5 oz)

2 teaspoons sesame seeds

salt and pepper

thyme sprigs, to garnish

• Don't waste time arranging the filo neatly. Just make sure the pastry covers the filling so it doesn't dry out during baking.
• If possible buy fresh filo so that you can then freeze the leftover pastry. If you use frozen filo, the rest of the packet will keep in the refrigerator for a couple of days.
• Lean minced lamb can be used instead of fillet.

Trim the lamb of any fat and cut into pieces. Process briefly in a food processor until chopped into small pieces.

Heat 2 tablespoons of the oil in a large frying pan or sauté pan. Add the lamb, aubergine and onions and fry, stirring, for 5–10 minutes until browned.

Add the garlic, tomatoes, tomato paste, red peppers, courgettes, thyme and a little salt and pepper and bring just to the boil. Reduce the heat, cover the pan and cook gently for 20 minutes until the lamb is tender and the sauce is pulpy. Turn into a shallow 1.8 litre (3 pint) pie dish.

On a clean work surface, crumple up one filo sheet roughly to the dimensions of the pie dish and brush with a little oil. Crumple another sheet over this one and brush with more oil. Crumple the final filo sheet on top. Carefully lift the pastry over the filling, easing it to fit so the edges just cover the rim of the pie dish.

Brush with any remaining oil and scatter with the sesame seeds. Bake in a preheated oven at 200°C (400°F) Gas Mark 6 for about 20 minutes until the pastry is golden. Serve garnished with thyme.

BONUS POINT
• Combining plenty of vegetables with a modest amount of lean meat creates a good nutritional balance, as well as keeping down costs. This recipe is a complete meal, although, for larger appetites, you might want to serve it with some grainy bread.

PORK AND APPLE MEATBALLS WITH LINGUINI

These simple meatballs are whizzed together in a food processor and oven baked, so they cook without your constant attention. Don't worry about forming them into neat shapes; just scoop even-sized spoonfuls on to the baking sheet. Flavour the mixture with a tablespoonful of chopped fresh sage if you like, though very young children might find the flavour too strong.

Preparation time: 20 minutes **Cooking time:** 25 minutes

1 onion, roughly chopped
500 g (1 lb) lean minced pork
1 tablespoon plain flour
1 teaspoon English mustard
4 dessert apples, peeled, cored and
    roughly chopped
250 g (8 oz) dried linguini, tagliatelle or
    spaghetti
400 g (13 oz) spring greens or cabbage
2 tablespoons olive oil
salt and pepper

Put the onion in a food processor with the pork, flour, mustard and a little salt and pepper. Blend in short bursts until the onion is finely chopped, then add half of the apples and blend until the mixture holds together.

Using 2 teaspoons, scoop the mixture into rough balls and place on a lightly oiled baking sheet. Bake in a preheated oven at 200°C (400°F) Gas Mark 6 for 25 minutes until firm and beginning to colour.

Meanwhile, cook the pasta in plenty of boiling salted water for 10 minutes or until just tender.

While the pasta is cooking, shred the spring greens or cabbage as finely as possible. Heat the oil in a frying pan and fry the greens until tender, about 5 minutes. Add the remaining apples and cook for a further 2 minutes.

Lightly drain the pasta and return to the pan. Add the greens, apples and a little salt and pepper and toss to mix. Spoon on to warmed serving plates, pile the meatballs on top and serve immediately.

BONUS POINTS
• Cabbage is an excellent source of many vitamins and minerals, especially vitamins C, E and K. It is also thought to have cancer-inhibiting properties. Tossing shredded cabbage with pasta is a good way to disguise this vegetable for children who aren't keen on it.
• Buy organic apples so that you don't have to peel them before use. An apple's vitamins are most concentrated just under the skin, so a significant proportion of these is lost on peeling.

ONE-POT PORK ROAST

A quick and easy mid-week roast, comprising pork chops and plenty of root vegetables – all cooked in one pan for convenience. If you have time, poach some dessert apples in a dash of water to serve with the pork.

Preparation time: 15 minutes **Cooking time:** 1 hour

4 pork chops

6 fresh sage leaves, chopped

2 teaspoons grainy mustard

grated rind and juice of ½ lemon

2 garlic cloves, crushed

4 tablespoons olive oil

3 baking potatoes

400 g (13 oz) parsnips

400 g (13 oz) carrots

salt and pepper

• Make a quick gravy from the roasting juices if you like. Transfer the meat and vegetables to serving plates, using a slotted spoon. Add 300 ml (½ pint) stock (or half stock and half white wine) to the roasting tin and bubble on the hob to reduce, stirring to incorporate the cooking juices.
• For more adventurous tastes use root vegetables such as beetroot, turnip, celeriac and sweet potatoes.

Trim the fat from the pork. Mix together the sage leaves, mustard, lemon rind and juice, garlic, a dash of the oil, and salt and pepper. Brush over the pork chops and set aside.

Peel the potatoes and cut them into small roasting sized pieces. Peel the carrots and parsnips and cut them into wedges. Par-cook the vegetables in lightly salted boiling water for 5 minutes, then drain thoroughly.

Tip the vegetables into a large roasting tin, add the remaining olive oil and toss well. Roast in a preheated oven at 200°C (400°F) Gas Mark 6 for 15 minutes.

Add the pork chops to the roasting tin and return to the oven for a further 35–40 minutes until they are cooked through and the vegetables are lightly browned. Serve with a green vegetable like broccoli, French beans or cabbage.

BONUS POINTS
• Carrots are a rich source of beta-carotene, which is converted into vitamin A in the body. Vitamin A is essential for eye function, immunity, growth and cell maintenance.
• Parsnips aid bowel functioning and detoxify and cleanse the digestive tract.

INDONESIAN BEEF NOODLES

This tasty, soupy noodle dish features a number of flavouring ingredients but the method is very quick. Lean, tender beef is used, though you can substitute boneless chicken breast or pork fillet if you prefer.

Preparation time: 15 minutes **Cooking time:** 10 minutes

250 g (8 oz) fine rice noodles or ribbon noodles

375 g (12 oz) lean steak

2 tablespoons sunflower or vegetable oil

3 garlic cloves, sliced

1 bunch of spring onions, trimmed and roughly chopped

5 cm (2 inch) piece fresh root ginger, grated

4 tablespoons peanut butter

1 tablespoon dark soy sauce

finely grated rind and juice of 1 lime

1 teaspoon light muscovado sugar

900 ml (1½ pints) chicken stock

50 g (2 oz) roasted cashew nuts

100 g (3½ oz) mangetout, halved

Cook or soak the noodles according to the packet directions; drain.

Meanwhile, trim the beef of any fat, then cut it into very thin strips. Heat the oil in a wok or large saucepan. Add the beef and fry quickly for 2 minutes. Remove with a slotted spoon and set aside.

Add the garlic, spring onions and ginger to the pan and fry for 1 minute. Add the peanut butter, soy sauce, lime rind and juice, sugar and stock and bring to the boil. Reduce the heat, cover the pan and cook gently for 5 minutes.

Return the beef to the pan and add the noodles, cashew nuts and mangetout. Cook gently for 2 minutes. Serve immediately in warmed bowls or shallow serving dishes.

BONUS POINTS

• Nuts such as cashews and peanuts are rich in protein, fibre, vitamins, minerals and essential fatty acids. However, as they are high in fat, they should be eaten in moderation. Children under the age of 5 should not be given whole nuts because of the risk of choking.

• Stir-frying is a healthier alternative to other frying methods, as minimal oil is used and the cooking is very fast.

• Always trim as much fat as possible from meat before cooking.

• As peanut butter, soy sauce and stock (if seasoned) all provide salt, you probably won't need additional salt in this recipe.

• Rice noodles are made from rice flour and water and are available dried from larger supermarkets, usually in ribbon form. Fine egg noodles can be used instead.

Vegetarian Meals

The ever-increasing range of exciting ingredients in shops, combined with an interest in foods discovered abroad, has taken most families beyond the realms of a 'meat and two veg' diet. Vegetarian meals are nutritionally sound and incorporate interesting ingredients and cooking techniques that may inspire the whole family, vegetarian or not.

ROASTED VEGETABLES WITH CHEESE

Roasted vegetables are delicious on their own, but even better tossed with tangy cheese and a sweet honey dressing, to make a simple, light meal. Serve with a green salad and warm ciabatta or crusty, grainy bread. You may prefer to scatter toddler portions with a familiar cheese, such as Emmenthal or Cheddar instead of halloumi.

Preparation time: 15 minutes **Cooking time:** 35 minutes

2 sweet potatoes, about 500 g (1 lb)

2 small red onions, cut into wedges

2 red peppers, cored, deseeded and cut into wedges

1 yellow pepper, cored, deseeded and cut into wedges

3 courgettes, cut into chunks

5 tablespoons olive oil

1 garlic clove, crushed

finely grated rind and juice of 1 lemon

2 tablespoons clear honey

200 g (7 oz) halloumi or feta cheese, drained and diced

salt and pepper

lemon wedges, to serve (optional)

Scrub the sweet potatoes, slice thinly and put them into a large roasting tin with the onions, peppers and courgettes. Add 2 tablespoons of the oil and toss the ingredients together. Roast the vegetables in a preheated oven at 200°C (400°F) Gas Mark 6 for about 30 minutes until they are golden, tossing them once or twice during roasting.

Meanwhile, mix together the remaining oil, the garlic, lemon rind and juice, honey and salt and pepper.

Scatter the cheese over the vegetables and cook for a further 5 minutes. Transfer to warmed serving plates, spoon on the dressing, and serve with lemon wedges, if wished. Accompany with a salad and warm bread.

BONUS POINTS
• Plant pigments in the vegetables act as antioxidants in the body, helping to protect cells from damage.
• Cheese is a rich source of protein and provides plenty of calcium, which is essential for growing bones and teeth and helps nerves and muscles function smoothly.

CHEESEBURGERS WITH JACKET CHIPS

Served with mildly spiced, wholesome homemade chips, these simple cheeseburgers make a great family meal. They are also a useful freezer standby for vegetarians when others are having fish or meat burgers. Serve with salad and a lemony mayonnaise, or the kids' favourite – ketchup!

Preparation time: 20 minutes **Cooking time:** 30 minutes

Jacket chips:

1 kg (2 lb) baking potatoes

3 tablespoons vegetable oil

1 teaspoon each of ground cumin, coriander and chilli powder

Cheeseburgers:

400 g (13 oz) can red kidney beans, rinsed and drained

1 small onion, finely chopped

100 g (3½ oz) mature Cheddar cheese, grated

100 g (3½ oz) white or brown breadcrumbs

1 egg

1 tablespoon vegetable oil

salt and pepper

• Other canned beans – such as haricot, cannellini, or borlotti – can be used instead of kidney beans.

• For a tasty condiment to serve with the burgers, mix equal quantities of mayonnaise and Greek yogurt with a little mustard, grated lemon rind or crushed garlic.

To make the chips, scrub the potatoes and cut them into small wedges. Pat them dry on kitchen paper and put in a roasting tin. Drizzle with the oil and sprinkle with the spices. Roast in a preheated oven at 220°C (425°F) Gas Mark 7 for about 30 minutes until golden, turning the potatoes once or twice during roasting.

Meanwhile, make the burgers. Put the beans in a bowl and mash with a fork to break them up. Add the onion, cheese, breadcrumbs, egg and salt and pepper, and mix to a smooth paste.

Using floured hands, shape the mixture into 4 rounds, then flatten them into cakes. Heat the oil in a frying pan and fry the burgers gently for 8–10 minutes, turning once, until crisp and golden. Serve with the jacket chips.

BONUS POINT

• These homemade oven chips are a healthier alternative to bought oven chips, as they're much lower in calories and fat. They contain far less than half the fat and calories of traditional deep-fried chips.

CHICKPEA & MUSHROOM SAUSAGES

Whizzed up in a food processor, these delicious sausages are surprisingly quick and easy. Serve them with a green vegetable such as broccoli or cabbage, and mashed potatoes or noodles.

Preparation time: 15 minutes **Cooking time:** 20 minutes

3 large red onions

3 tablespoons olive oil

250 g (8 oz) chestnut mushrooms, roughly sliced

½ teaspoon medium curry paste

400 g (13 oz) can chickpeas, drained

finely grated rind of 1 lemon

75 g (3 oz) white or brown breadcrumbs

1 teaspoon caster sugar

salt and pepper

Thinly slice 2 of the onions and set aside. Roughly chop the other onion. Heat 1 tablespoon of the oil in a frying pan. Add the chopped onion and fry for 3 minutes. Add the mushrooms and fry for about 5 minutes until they are golden and any moisture has evaporated.

Transfer the mixture to a food processor and add the curry paste, chickpeas, lemon rind and salt and pepper to taste. Work to a coarse paste, then add the breadcrumbs and process lightly until evenly combined.

Using lightly floured hands, shape the mixture into 10–12 sausages and place on a baking sheet. (The paste will be soft, but firms up during cooking.)

Heat 1 tablespoon of the oil in a frying pan. Add the sliced onions with the sugar and fry gently for 10 minutes or until golden and caramelized. Meanwhile, brush the sausages with the remaining oil and cook under a preheated moderate grill for about 10 minutes, turning frequently until evenly golden. Serve with the caramelized onions.

BONUS POINTS
• Mushrooms contain protein, potassium and riboflavin. They are believed to have other healthy properties too, such as helping to lower blood cholesterol levels.
• Pulses such as chickpeas are a good source of protein, fibre, minerals and B vitamins. They are particularly valuable in a vegetarian diet.

• If you do not have a food processor, pulp the chickpeas and mushroom mixture together in a blender, then transfer to a bowl and mix with the breadcrumbs.

STUFFED VEGETABLES WITH COUSCOUS

Peppers and large tomatoes make perfect containers for savoury stuffings and roast to a sweet tenderness, which children appreciate too. Use a mixture of peppers and tomatoes or stick to one, depending on your family's preference. Serve with a leafy salad and warm bread.

Preparation time: 15 minutes **Cooking time:** 30 minutes

2 beefsteak tomatoes

2 red, orange or yellow peppers

2 tablespoons olive oil

175 g (6 oz) couscous

300 ml (½ pint) boiling water

½ bunch of spring onions, trimmed and chopped

small handful of basil leaves, torn into pieces

125 g (4 oz) mozzarella cheese, drained and chopped

25 g (1 oz) Parmesan cheese, freshly grated

400 g (13 oz) can chickpeas, rinsed and drained

salt and pepper

Halve the tomatoes horizontally and scoop out the pulp and seeds. Halve the peppers lengthways and discard the core and seeds. Put the tomatoes and peppers, cup-side up, in a large shallow ovenproof dish and drizzle with the oil and a little salt and pepper. Bake in a preheated oven at 200°C (400°F) Gas Mark 6 for 20 minutes until softened.

Meanwhile, put the couscous in a bowl, pour on the boiling water and leave to stand for 10 minutes until the water is absorbed. Fluff up the couscous with a fork and stir in the spring onions, basil, mozzarella, Parmesan, chickpeas and season with salt and pepper to taste.

Spoon the couscous mixture into the baked vegetables and return the dish to the oven for a further 8–10 minutes until the vegetables have heated through and the mozzarella has melted. Serve warm, with salad and warmed bread.

BONUS POINT
• Parmesan cheese is a valid inclusion in a healthy diet, as a small amount provides plenty of flavour without adding too much fat.

• Chickpeas add texture and flavour but they can be left out, or replaced with a sprinkling of toasted pine nuts if preferred.
• Mozzarella gives a lovely melting texture, while Parmesan adds plenty of flavour. Finely diced mature Cheddar can be substituted for a more economical version.

SPANISH VEGETABLE STEW

A cross between a chunky soup and a cassoulet, this delicious stew is packed with a colourful assortment of vegetables. It can be cooked on the hob or – for convenience – left to slowly stew in the oven so it's ready and waiting for the breadcrumb topping whenever you are.

Preparation time: 15 minutes **Cooking time:** 45 minutes

3 tablespoons olive oil

2 onions, thinly sliced

3 garlic cloves, sliced

1 tablespoon paprika

1 green pepper, cored, deseeded and sliced

1 red or orange pepper, cored, deseeded and sliced

25 g (1 oz) butter

50 g (2 oz) coarse breadcrumbs

500 g (1 lb) potatoes, cut into chunks

2 tablespoons tomato purée

600 ml (1 pint) vegetable stock

2 x 400 g (13 oz) cans butter beans, rinsed and drained

200 g (7 oz) baby spinach or shredded spring greens

Heat the oil in a large saucepan or flameproof casserole. Add the onions, garlic, paprika and sliced peppers and fry very gently for 6–8 minutes until softened and browned.

Meanwhile, melt the butter in a separate pan and fry the breadcrumbs for 2 minutes or until golden.

Add the potatoes, tomato purée and stock to the pepper mixture and bring just to the boil. Reduce the heat, cover the pan and simmer very gently for about 30 minutes until the vegetables are tender.

Stir in the butter beans and spinach or spring greens and cook for 3–4 minutes until the butter beans have heated through and the spinach has wilted. Sprinkle with the breadcrumbs to serve.

BONUS POINTS
• The soluble fibre in the vegetables and butter beans helps prevent constipation and lower the blood cholesterol level.
• Spinach, spring greens and other dark green vegetables are good sources of carotenoids, vitamin C and potassium. They also contain useful amounts of folate and iron.

• Ring the changes with different root and green vegetables. Parsnips, turnips, celeriac, shredded greens and courgettes are all suitable.
• Cook the stew in the oven at 180°C (350°F) Gas Mark 4, if preferred.

CHUNKY CARROT & LENTIL SOUP

This nutritious soup is substantial enough for a main course if you serve it with some good grainy bread. A zesty, spiced butter, stirred in at the table, adds a livelier flavour for older children and adults.

Preparation time: 10 minutes **Cooking time:** 30–35 minutes

2 tablespoons vegetable oil
1 large onion, chopped
2 celery sticks, sliced
500 g (1 lb) carrots, sliced
1 garlic clove, crushed
150 g (5 oz) split red lentils, rinsed
1.4 litres (2¼ pints) vegetable stock
salt and pepper

Spiced butter (optional):
40 g (1½ oz) lightly salted butter, softened
2 spring onions, trimmed and finely chopped
¼ teaspoon dried chilli flakes
1 teaspoon cumin seeds, lightly crushed
finely grated rind of 1 lemon
small handful of coriander, chopped
several mint sprigs, chopped

• If you omit the spicy butter, serve the soup topped with toasted French bread and cheese, for a robust meal.
• Wrap any leftover spiced butter in clingfilm, refrigerate and use as a topping for jacket potatoes.

First make the spiced butter, if serving. Put all the ingredients in a bowl and beat together until combined. Transfer to a small serving dish, cover and chill until ready to serve.

To make the soup, heat the oil in a large saucepan. Add the onion and celery and cook gently for 5 minutes until softened. Add the carrots and garlic and fry for 3 minutes.

Add the lentils and stock and bring just to the boil. Reduce the heat, cover the pan and cook gently for 20–25 minutes until the vegetables are soft and the soup is pulpy. Season lightly to taste with salt and pepper.

Divide the soup between warmed bowls. Serve the spiced butter, if using, at the table, so diners can stir in as much as they like.

BONUS POINTS
• Like wholegrain bread, cereals and starchy vegetables, lentils are a source of complex carbohydrate. This is digested and absorbed more slowly than simple sugars to provide sustained energy over a longer period of time.
• Carrots are high in pectin, a soluble fibre which helps to prevent some toxins being absorbed into the body. Pectin also helps to balance blood sugar levels and lower blood cholesterol.

WARM COLESLAW SALAD

This simple supper dish is a delicious update on a traditional coleslaw. A food processor makes light work of preparing the vegetables. Serve with wholemeal or grainy bread, or pasta if you prefer.

Preparation time: 15 minutes **Cooking time:** 5 minutes

½ small red cabbage, about 400 g
    (13 oz), cut into wedges
1 red onion, roughly chopped
200 g (7 oz) mangetout or runner beans,
    trimmed
2 small raw beetroot, peeled and cut
    into wedges
2 tablespoons walnut or sunflower oil
50 g (2 oz) walnut pieces
200 g (7 oz) peeled prawns, defrosted
    and drained if frozen
salt and pepper

Red pepper mayonnaise:

1 red pepper, cored, deseeded and
    roughly chopped
6 tablespoons mayonnaise
1 tablespoon tomato purée
1 teaspoon paprika
salt and pepper

First prepare the red pepper mayonnaise. Finely chop the pepper in a food processor. Turn into a bowl and stir in the mayonnaise, tomato purée, paprika and a little salt and pepper. Transfer to a serving bowl and chill.

To make the coleslaw, fit the food processor with the slicer attachment and use to slice the cabbage, onion, and mangetout or beans. Switch to the shredder attachment and shred the beetroot.

Heat the oil in a large frying pan or wok. Add the cabbage mixture and walnuts and stir-fry gently for 3–4 minutes until heated through. Season lightly to taste. Transfer one portion to a warmed serving plate.

Add the prawns to the pan, stir-fry for 1 minute, then transfer to the other warmed serving plates.

Serve the warm salad at once, topped with the red pepper mayonnaise.

BONUS POINTS
• Light cooking ensures that most of the valuable nutrients in this coleslaw are retained.
• Beetroot is a good source of folate, vitamin C, calcium, potassium and other important minerals. It is also thought to have detoxifying properties.

• Hazelnuts or almonds can be used instead of walnuts.
• For a lighter dressing, use half Greek yogurt and half mayonnaise.
• If preferred, replace the prawns with thinly sliced lean chicken, turkey, beef or pork. Stir-fry in a separate pan until cooked through before adding to the coleslaw.

WHOLEWHEAT SALAD WITH CHILLI TOMATOES

Wholewheat grains make an excellent base for a main course salad, and are a welcome change from the more usual pasta, potatoes or rice. Wheat, pine nuts and cheese provide ample protein for vegetarians, while grilled lamb chops are an easy addition for meat eaters.

Preparation time: 15 minutes **Cooking time:** 20 minutes

250 g (8 oz) pre-cooked wholewheat grains

6 lamb cutlets

750 g (1½ lb) vine tomatoes

3 tablespoons olive oil

3 tablespoons balsamic vinegar

1 mild red chilli, cored, deseeded and thinly sliced

4 tablespoons snipped chives, or 2 spring onions, finely chopped

50 g (2 oz) pine nuts

50 g (2 oz) rocket or baby spinach

1 small red onion, cut into rings

50 g (2 oz) feta, Cheddar or Cheshire cheese, crumbled

salt and pepper

Cook the wholewheat in plenty of lightly salted boiling water for 20 minutes or until tender.

While the wheat is cooking, trim the lamb of any excess fat and season it lightly on both sides with salt and pepper. When the wholewheat is almost cooked, put the lamb on a grill rack under a preheated high grill and cook for 5 minutes on each side.

Meanwhile, quarter the tomatoes. Scoop the seeds and pulp into a sieve over a large bowl and press with the back of a spoon to extract the juice. Add the tomato quarters and their juice to the bowl with the oil, vinegar, chilli and salt and pepper to taste.

Drain the wholewheat and return it to the pan. Add the chives or spring onions, pine nuts, rocket or spinach, and a little salt and pepper. Spoon on to serving plates and top with the tomato mixture and the red onion rings. Add the grilled cutlets to 3 servings and sprinkle the crumbled cheese over the vegetarian portion.

BONUS POINT
• Wholewheat provides good quality carbohydrate as well as B vitamins, calcium and other minerals.

• Healthfood stores and selected supermarkets sell wholewheat grains. 'Pre-cooked' brands cook more quickly than raw grains, which also require pre-soaking.

• Allow an extra 3 minutes each side if you prefer lamb well cooked.

• Grilled steak, salmon or sardines can be substituted for the lamb.

Freeze-ahead

Take a little time to prepare and freeze a selection of main meals and you will always have a source of instant, nutritious meals. Freezer standbys are invaluable for midweek meals – especially if you are working and have no time to shop or cook. Accompanying vegetables form an integral part of some dishes – serving these couldn't be simpler.

SAVOURY FISH PIE

Cooked fish only freezes well if it's bathed in sauce to keep it moist – as in this recipe. Flavoured with leeks and blue cheese, this tasty pie is a meal in itself, though you could serve it with a vegetable or leafy salad. **Serves 4–5**

Preparation time: 25 minutes   **Cooking time:** 10 minutes   **Reheating time:** 50 minutes

750 g (1½ lb) potatoes
750 g (1½ lb) cod or haddock fillet
350 ml (12 fl oz) semi-skimmed milk
25 g (1 oz) butter
500 g (1 lb) leeks, sliced
2 tablespoons plain white flour
125 g (4 oz) blue cheese, crumbled
plenty of freshly grated nutmeg
salt and pepper
watercress sprigs, to garnish

• Only freeze this pie if you use fish that hasn't been frozen previously.
• If preferred, use grated Cheddar instead of blue cheese.
• To accentuate the golden topping, sprinkle with 2 tablespoons grated Cheddar and a little finely crumbled blue cheese before baking.

Scrub the potatoes and slice them thinly. Cook in a saucepan of lightly salted boiling water for 8–10 minutes until tender. Drain.

Meanwhile, put the fish in a large frying pan and pour on a third of the milk. Cover the pan and simmer gently for 6–8 minutes until cooked through. Lift the fish on to a plate; pour the cooking liquid into a jug and reserve.

Wipe out the pan, then melt the butter. Add the leeks and cook until softened. Stir in the flour and cook, stirring, for 1 minute. Gradually blend in the reserved cooking liquid and the remaining milk, whisking until the sauce has thickened. Add the cheese and stir until melted. Season with nutmeg, salt and pepper.

Put the leeks in a 1.8 litre (3 pint) pie dish. Roughly flake the fish, checking for bones, then scatter over the leeks. Pour on half of the sauce. Layer the potato slices over the filling, then pour on the remaining sauce.

Leave the pie until cold, then cover it with foil and freeze for up to 2 months; or refrigerate for up to 24 hours.

To thaw: transfer to the refrigerator 24 hours before serving.

To serve: bake in a preheated oven at 180°C (350°F) Gas Mark 4 for about 50 minutes until golden and bubbling. Serve garnished with watercress.

BONUS POINT
• Fish, milk and cheese provide plenty of calcium and protein.

NORTH AFRICAN FISH STEW

Richly flavoured with spices and tomatoes, this quick and easy fish stew is best served with rice, or generous chunks of grainy bread for mopping up the delicious juices. **Serves 4–6**

Preparation time: 15 minutes **Cooking time:** 8 minutes **Reheating time:** 10 minutes

500 g (1 lb) cod or haddock fillet
3 tablespoons olive oil
250 g (8 oz) squid rings (see note)
2 small red onions, chopped
1 small fennel bulb, or 2 celery sticks, chopped
3 garlic cloves, sliced
2 tablespoons paprika
1 tablespoon cumin seeds
½ teaspoon dried chilli flakes
4 tablespoons sun-dried tomato paste
900 ml (1½ pints) fish or vegetable stock
400 g (13 oz) can black beans or red kidney beans, rinsed and drained

To serve:
small handful of coriander leaves
small handful of mint sprigs

Cut the white fish into chunks, discarding any skin and residual bones. Heat the oil in a large frying pan or saucepan. Add the white fish and squid rings and fry gently for 2 minutes; remove with a slotted spoon and set aside.

Add the onions, fennel or celery, garlic and spices to the pan and fry for 3 minutes. Add the tomato paste, stock, and black beans or kidney beans. Bring just to the boil, then remove the pan from the heat and add the fish.

Leave the stew until cold, then transfer it to a freezer container and freeze for up to 2 months; or refrigerate for up to 24 hours.

To thaw: transfer to the refrigerator 24 hours before serving.

To serve: tip the stew into a large saucepan and bring almost to the boil. Reduce the heat, cover and simmer gently for 10 minutes or until piping hot. Meanwhile, roughly chop the herbs. Serve the fish stew in warmed bowls, sprinkled with the herbs.

BONUS POINTS

• Extending the fish by including beans makes this dish more economical and substantial.
• Serving the stew with brown rice or grainy bread increases the carbohydrate content and adds fibre.

• Prepared squid is available from fishmongers and supermarket fresh fish counters. If the tentacles are included, do add them to the stew.
• The initial cooking time for the fish is brief because it continues to cook in the stock as it cools. It's important to avoid overcooking fish otherwise it will dry and toughen on reheating.

SMOKED FISH CRUMBLE

Savoury crumbles are great time-saving alternatives to traditional pies. They taste just as good and are much quicker to make, because there is no pastry to prepare – the crumble mixture is simply scattered over the filling. Serve with a green vegetable such as mangetout, broccoli or chard.

Preparation time: 15 minutes   **Cooking time:** 10 minutes   **Reheating time:** 45 minutes

500 g (1 lb) smoked cod or haddock fillet, skinned
2 tablespoons sunflower or vegetable oil
1 bunch of spring onions, trimmed and chopped
150 g (5 oz) chestnut mushrooms, sliced
1 tablespoon plain flour
250 ml (8 fl oz) semi-skimmed milk
3 tablespoons chopped fresh flat leaf parsley
2 tablespoons capers, rinsed (optional)
grated rind of 1 lemon
pepper

Crumble:
100 g (3½ oz) plain white flour
75 g (3 oz) butter, cut into small pieces
50 g (2 oz) porridge oats

Cut the fish into 2 cm (¾ inch) chunks, checking for any residual bones. Heat the oil in a large frying pan. Add the spring onions and mushrooms and fry for 3 minutes. Add the flour and cook, stirring, for 1 minute. Gradually blend in the milk.

Add the fish and cook gently for about 5 minutes, stirring until the sauce has thickened. Remove from the heat and stir in the parsley, the capers, if using, lemon rind and pepper. Turn into a 1.5 litre (2½ pint) shallow ovenproof pie dish and leave to cool.

To make the crumble, put the flour in a food processor, add the butter and process until the mixture resembles breadcrumbs. Add the oats and process briefly to combine.

Scatter the crumble over the filling. Cover with foil and freeze for up to 3 months; or refrigerate for up to 24 hours.

To thaw: transfer the pie to the refrigerator 24 hours before serving.

To serve: bake in a preheated oven at 190°C (375°F) Gas Mark 5 for about 45 minutes until the crumble is golden.

BONUS POINTS

• Including oats in the crumble, rather than using all flour, provides extra fibre that helps to lower blood cholesterol levels.
• The high protein content of fish is not affected when it is smoked.

• Make sure you buy naturally smoked, creamy coloured cod or haddock. Avoid bright yellow smoked fish – this is coloured and smoked artificially, and lacks a genuine 'smoky' flavour.

CHICKEN & SPINACH PIE

Chunks of chicken, fresh spinach, ginger and creamed coconut combine to make an unusual but delicious filling under a mashed potato topping. An interesting alternative to shepherd's pie, for children with adventurous tastes. Serve with a green vegetable, such as broccoli or peas, if liked.

Preparation time: 20 minutes   **Cooking time:** 15 minutes   **Reheating time:** 50 minutes

2 tablespoons sunflower or vegetable oil

1 onion, chopped

3 garlic cloves, sliced

4 cm (1½ inch) piece fresh root ginger

6 boneless, skinless chicken thighs, cut into chunks

300 ml (½ pint) chicken stock

75 g (3 oz) creamed coconut (from a block)

875 g (1¾ lb) potatoes, peeled and cut into pieces

5 tablespoons semi-skimmed milk

150 g (5 oz) fresh spinach, trimmed

plenty of freshly grated nutmeg

salt and pepper

Heat the oil in a large frying pan or sauté pan. Add the onion, garlic, ginger and chicken pieces and fry gently for about 5 minutes until the chicken is just beginning to colour.

Add the stock and creamed coconut and bring to a simmer, stirring gently to blend the coconut into the liquid. Cover and cook gently for 10 minutes.

Meanwhile, cook the potatoes in lightly salted boiling water for about 15 minutes until soft. Drain, return to the pan and mash with the milk.

Pile the spinach on top of the chicken mixture and cover with a lid. Leave to cook gently for 1–2 minutes until the spinach has wilted. Add plenty of nutmeg and a little salt and pepper, and stir the spinach into the sauce.

Turn into a 1.8 litre (3 pint) pie dish. Top with the mashed potato and rough up the surface with a fork. Leave to cool. Cover with foil and freeze for up to 2 months; or refrigerate for up to 24 hours.

To thaw: transfer to the refrigerator 24 hours before serving.

To serve: bake the pie in a preheated oven at 180°C (350°F) Gas Mark 4 for about 50 minutes until the surface is pale golden.

BONUS POINTS

• Fresh ginger aids digestion, helps to alleviate stomach upsets, and improves circulation.

• Spinach is a nutritious vegetable, rich in beta-carotene and vitamin C, and a useful source of folate, iron and potassium. However, it is not exceptionally high in iron as was once thought.

• Creamed coconut – sold in blocks – has a more concentrated flavour than canned coconut milk, or coconut cream that is usually sold in cartons. Solid when cold, creamed coconut can become quite soft during hot weather – don't be put off by this when buying. As well as adding an exotic flavour, creamed coconut acts as a natural thickener in sauces.

CHICKEN WITH LEMONS & OLIVES

A Mediterranean-style dish with the vibrant flavours of lemon, basil and olives. The olives and basil are stirred in shortly before serving, so it's easy to exclude them for children who aren't keen on their distinctive flavours. Serve with rice or couscous, and a leafy salad.

Preparation time: 15 minutes **Cooking time:** 40 minutes **Reheating time:** 20 minutes

1 large lemon
3 tablespoons olive oil
8 skinless chicken thighs
4 garlic cloves, sliced
1 tablespoon plain flour
300 ml (½ pint) chicken stock
salt and pepper

To finish:
3 tablespoons crème fraîche
small handful of basil leaves, shredded
8–10 pitted black olives

Cut the lemon into 8 wedges, discarding any visible seeds.

Heat the oil in a large saucepan or flameproof casserole. Add the chicken thighs and fry gently for 5 minutes until pale golden. Add the lemon wedges and garlic and fry for 2 minutes. Take out the lemon wedges and cut them into slices; set aside.

Add the flour to the pan and cook, stirring, for 1 minute. Stir in the stock and return the lemon slices to the pan. Bring just to the boil, then reduce the heat. Cover the pan and simmer gently for 30 minutes until the chicken is cooked through. Check the seasoning.

Leave to cool. Transfer to a freezer container and freeze for up to 3 months; or refrigerate for up to 24 hours.

To thaw: transfer to the refrigerator 24 hours before serving.

To serve: turn into a large pan and bring to a simmer. Cover and cook gently for 20 minutes or until piping hot. Stir in the crème fraîche, shredded basil and olives. Heat through for 1 minute before serving.

BONUS POINTS
• Chicken is an excellent source of protein. It also contains B vitamins, zinc and some iron. Cooking chicken portions without the skin considerably reduces the amount of fat.
• Lemons are an excellent source of vitamin C, which is essential for a healthy immune system.

• Lemons are generally coated with wax which is difficult to remove by washing. Buy organic, unwaxed lemons for this dish, and whenever the rind is included in a recipe.
• To cook the couscous, put 250 g (8 oz) couscous in a bowl, pour on 300 ml (½ pint) boiling water or stock, cover and leave in a warm place for 10–15 minutes until the liquid is absorbed. Fluff up with a fork to serve.

MEXICAN CHILLI

This richly flavoured chilli, made with pork and red peppers, is moderately spiced to appeal to the whole family. It's worth doubling up the quantities and freezing half of it in single portions for those occasions when you need a single meal, or have an extra person to feed.

Preparation time: 15 minutes **Cooking time:** 25 minutes **Reheating time:** 20 minutes

2 tablespoons sunflower or vegetable oil

1 large onion, chopped

2 garlic cloves, crushed

½ teaspoon dried chilli flakes

2 teaspoons paprika

500 g (1 lb) lean pork mince

2 red peppers, cored, deseeded and chopped

400 g (13 oz) can chopped tomatoes

2 teaspoons light muscovado sugar

300 ml (½ pint) chicken or vegetable stock

400 g (13 oz) can red kidney beans, rinsed and drained

To serve:

chopped flat leaf parsley or coriander (optional)

Greek yogurt

Heat the oil in a saucepan. Add the onion and fry gently for 5 minutes. Add the garlic, spices and pork and fry for 5 minutes, breaking up the pork with a wooden spoon.

Add the red peppers, tomatoes, sugar and stock and bring to the boil. Reduce the heat, cover the pan and simmer gently for 15 minutes. Remove the pan from the heat and leave to cool.

Stir in the red kidney beans and turn into a freezer container. Freeze for up to 3 months; or refrigerate for up to 24 hours.

To thaw: transfer to the refrigerator 24 hours before serving.

To serve: place in a large saucepan and bring just to the boil. Reduce the heat, cover and simmer gently for 20 minutes until pulpy and very hot. Scatter with fresh herbs, if liked, and serve with spoonfuls of Greek yogurt.

BONUS POINT
• Red peppers are very high in vitamin C and beta-carotene, both of which are important immune boosters and may have anti-ageing properties.

• Chicken or turkey mince can be used instead of pork if preferred.
• Be cautious with dried chilli flakes the first time you use a new jar or pack. Brands vary in 'heat' and some can be very fiery.

BEEF WITH COLCANNON

This rich, beefy stew – zipped up with interesting flavours like pickled walnuts and port – makes a warming, wintry dish that can be frozen ahead and eaten at your leisure. The walnuts can be removed easily from children's portions if required. **Serves 6**

Preparation time: 25 minutes **Cooking time:** about 1 hour **Reheating time:** 25 minutes

1 kg (2 lb) lean casserole steak

2 tablespoons plain flour

2 tablespoons sunflower or vegetable oil

2 onions, chopped

750 ml (1¼ pints) beef stock

150 ml (¼ pint) port (or additional stock)

3 bay leaves

4 pickled walnuts, quartered

Colcannon:

1 kg (2 lb) baking potatoes, peeled and
    cut into chunks

500 g (1 lb) Savoy cabbage or spring
    greens, roughly shredded

25 g (1 oz) butter

1 onion, chopped

4 tablespoons semi-skimmed milk

salt and pepper

• The alcohol is burnt off during cooking, so this dish is suitable for children. However, you can use extra stock instead if preferred.

• The beef stew and vegetable accompaniment involve some preparation, but reheating and serving are then effortless.

Cut the beef into small chunks, discarding any excess fat. Season the flour with salt and pepper and use to coat the meat. Heat the oil in a large heavy-based saucepan, add half the beef and fry quickly until browned. Remove with a slotted spoon and fry the remainder.

Return all the beef to the pan with the onions and fry for 2 minutes. Add the stock, the port, if using, and bay leaves. Bring just to the boil. Lower the heat, cover the pan and simmer very gently for 1 hour or until the beef is tender.

In the meantime, make the colcannon. Cook the potatoes in a large pan of lightly salted boiling water until tender, about 20 minutes. Add the cabbage to the pan and cook for a further 5 minutes. Meanwhile, melt the butter in a small pan, add the onion and fry for 5 minutes.

Drain the potato and cabbage thoroughly and return to the saucepan. Add the onion and milk and mash well. Turn into a 1.5 litre (2½ pint) shallow ovenproof freezer dish. Fluff up the surface with a fork and leave to cool.

Leave the beef to cool, then stir in the pickled walnuts. Turn into a freezer container. Freeze the beef and colcannon separately for up to 3 months; or refrigerate for up to 24 hours.

To thaw: transfer the two dishes to the refrigerator 24 hours before serving.

To serve: bake the colcannon, uncovered, in a preheated oven at 190°C (375°F) Gas Mark 5 for 25 minutes or until heated through. Transfer the beef to a large pan and reheat gently for about 25 minutes until very hot.

BONUS POINT

• Beef is a very good source of 'haem iron' that is much more easily absorbed into the body than the 'non-haem iron' obtained from plant sources. Iron is required for transporting oxygen and carbon dioxide to and from cells.

LAMB BALTI

Spicy dishes invariably improve on reheating as their rich flavours have a second chance to mingle. This quick version of a balti uses curry paste with some whole spices to intensify and freshen the flavour. It's very easy to assemble if you have a good variety of spices in your storecupboard. Serve with naan bread or rice to mop up the juices, and some poppadums.

Preparation time: 20 minutes **Cooking time:** 50 minutes **Reheating time:** 25 minutes

625 g (1¼ lb) lean lamb fillet or leg

1 tablespoon freshly minced ginger
    (see note), drained

2 garlic cloves, crushed

150 ml (¼ pint) natural yogurt

12 cardamom pods

2 tablespoons sunflower or vegetable oil

2 large onions, cut into wedges

1 cinnamon stick, halved

1 teaspoon ground turmeric

1 teaspoon cumin seeds

2 bay leaves

2 teaspoons medium curry paste

250 g (8 oz) can chopped tomatoes

450 ml (¾ pint) lamb or chicken stock

625 g (1¼ lb) potatoes, peeled and cut
    into small chunks

3 tablespoons chopped coriander

salt and pepper

Cut the lamb into small chunks, discarding any fat. Put the lamb, ginger, garlic and yogurt in a heavy-based frying pan and heat until bubbling. Reduce the heat, cover the pan and simmer gently for 20 minutes.

Meanwhile, open the cardamom pods by gently pounding them with the end of a rolling pin to expose the seeds. Heat the oil in a saucepan, add the cardamoms, onions, cinnamon, turmeric, cumin and bay leaves and fry gently for 5 minutes.

Add the lamb mixture, curry paste, tomatoes and stock and bring to a simmer. Cover and cook for 15 minutes until the lamb is tender and the sauce has thickened slightly.

Add the potatoes to the pan and cook, covered, for a further 15 minutes until they are tender.

Leave to cool, then stir in the coriander. Turn into a freezer container and freeze for up to 3 months; or refrigerate for up to 24 hours.

To thaw: transfer to the refrigerator 24 hours before serving.

To serve: tip into a large saucepan and simmer gently, covered, for about 25 minutes until very hot.

BONUS POINTS

• Lamb is a high protein food and contains all of the essential amino acids – these are the 'building blocks' of the body. The essential ones are those that the body cannot make for itself.

• Using well-trimmed lean cuts of lamb, such as leg and fillet, cuts down on saturated fat consumption and lessens the risk of associated health problems such as heart disease and obesity.

• A jar of freshly minced ginger is a useful standby. Available from the supermarket spice section, it should be refrigerated after opening.

• On heating, the yogurt may look curdled, but it separates and thins to a delicious sauce as it cooks.

LAMB & LENTIL HOTPOT

Twice baking the lamb in this simple hotpot makes it deliciously succulent and tender. Lentils add plenty of extra goodness, but you can add more cutlets for big meat eaters if you need to.

Preparation time: 15 minutes **Cooking time:** 1 hour **Reheating time:** 45 minutes

100 g (3½ oz) green lentils, rinsed
8 lamb cutlets
2 tablespoons olive oil
2 onions, thinly sliced
2 garlic cloves, crushed
150 g (5 oz) chestnut mushrooms, sliced
several fresh rosemary sprigs
300 ml (½ pint) lamb or chicken stock
875 g (1¾ lb) potatoes, peeled
salt and pepper

• Unlike some beans and pulses, green lentils do not need soaking before use. Pre-boiling rapidly in water for 10 minutes before adding them to the casserole helps to remove any impurities.

Put the lentils in a small pan and cover with water. Bring to the boil and boil rapidly for 10 minutes. Drain and set aside.

Meanwhile, trim the lamb cutlets of any excess fat. Heat 1 tablespoon of the oil in a frying pan, add the cutlets and fry for 5 minutes, turning once, until browned. Transfer to a shallow 1.8 litre (3 pint) ovenproof dish.

Add the onions, garlic and mushrooms to the frying pan and fry for 3 minutes. Spoon over the lamb.

Add the lentils, rosemary, stock and a little salt and pepper to the pan and bring to the boil. Pour over the lamb.

Thinly slice the potatoes and layer over the lamb, seasoning the layers lightly. Drizzle with the remaining oil. Bake in a preheated oven at 180°C (350°F) Gas Mark 4 for 45 minutes or until the potatoes are turning pale golden. Leave to cool.

Cover the dish with foil and freeze for up to 3 months; or refrigerate for up to 24 hours.

To thaw: transfer to the refrigerator 24 hours before serving.

To serve: bake in a preheated oven at 180°C (350°F) Gas Mark 4 for 45 minutes until golden.

BONUS POINT
• Lentils are a highly nutritious food providing a good form of slow-release carbohydrate for sustained energy. They are also high in fibre, and a useful source of protein, minerals and B vitamins.

IRISH STEW

Cold weather and dark evenings put us in the mood for more traditional, comforting hot food, such as this chunky meat and vegetable stew.
Serves 4–5

Preparation time: 20 minutes **Cooking time:** 1¼ hours **Reheating time:** 25 minutes

750 g (1½ lb) lean fillet or leg of lamb
1 tablespoon plain flour
2 tablespoons sunflower or vegetable oil
3 onions, cut into wedges
400 g (13 oz) carrots, cut into chunks
875 g (1¾ lb) potatoes, scrubbed and
   quartered
900 ml (1½ pints) lamb or chicken stock
2 bay leaves
several fresh thyme sprigs
2 tablespoons Worcestershire sauce
salt and pepper

• Most stews benefit from freezing as gentle reheating further tenderizes the meat and accentuates the flavour.

Cut the lamb into even-sized cubes, discarding any excess fat. Season the flour with salt and pepper and use to coat the lamb.

Heat the oil in a large frying pan. Add the lamb and fry for 5–8 minutes until lightly browned. Remove the lamb with a slotted spoon and transfer to a casserole dish.

Add the onions and carrots to the frying pan and fry until lightly browned. Tip into the casserole with the potatoes.

Add the stock, herbs and Worcestershire sauce to the pan and bring to the boil. Pour into the casserole dish and season lightly. Cover and cook in a preheated oven at 180°C (350°F) Gas Mark 4 for 1 hour. Check the seasoning.

Leave to cool, then transfer to a freezer container and freeze for up to 3 months; or refrigerate for up to 24 hours.

To thaw: transfer to the refrigerator 24 hours before serving.

To serve: tip into a large saucepan and bring almost to the boil. Reduce the heat, cover the saucepan and simmer gently for 25 minutes or until very hot.

BONUS POINT
• Adding plenty of potatoes and vegetables to the stew provides a good balance of protein and carbohydrate.

Storecupboard

In this chapter the term storecupboard is used in the broadest sense to encompass ingredients that have a long shelf life, whether they're from the refrigerator, freezer or larder. With the inclusion of one or two fresh vegetables and herbs, basic items, such as canned tomatoes, beans, fish, frozen prawns, eggs and cheese, can be transformed into quick and easy main meals for days when you haven't the time, or energy, to shop.

TUNA KEDGEREE

250 g (8 oz) basmati rice

100 g (3½ oz) frozen baby broad beans

4 eggs

400 g (13 oz) can tuna in oil or brine, drained

25 g (1 oz) unsalted butter

1 small onion, finely chopped

1 teaspoon medium curry paste

small handful of flat leaf parsley, chopped

salt and pepper

flat leaf parsley sprigs, to garnish

lemon or lime wedges, to serve

> • Frozen sweetcorn or peas can be used instead of broad beans if preferred.
> • Other fresh herbs – such as tarragon, dill, coriander or chives – can be added with the parsley. If some family members aren't keen on these, add the extra herbs after serving their portions.

Canned tuna is such a useful storecupboard standby, not just as a sandwich filler, but for adding to pies, pizza toppings and jacket potatoes. Here it successfully takes the place of the more familiar smoked haddock.

Preparation time: 10 minutes **Cooking time:** about 15 minutes

Cook the rice in plenty of lightly salted boiling water for about 8 minutes until almost tender. Add the broad beans and cook for a further 3 minutes; drain.

Meanwhile, add the eggs to a pan of simmering water and simmer gently for 4–5 minutes. Drain and shell when cool enough to handle. Cut the boiled eggs into wedges. Flake the tuna into small chunks.

Melt the butter in a large frying pan, add the onion and curry paste and fry gently for 3 minutes. Add the drained rice and broad beans, with the tuna and eggs.

Stir in the parsley and season the kedgeree with salt and pepper to taste. Stir gently over a low heat for 1 minute, then transfer to serving plates. Garnish with parsley and serve with lemon or lime wedges.

BONUS POINTS
• Eggs are rich in protein, calcium, iron, zinc and B group vitamins. They are a concentrated source of nutrients and help promote good bones and joints. They also boost the immune system.
• Broad beans are a good source of slow-release carbohydrate that helps keep energy levels high.

SWEETCORN & PRAWN CHOWDER

The three main ingredients in this dish – sweetcorn, frozen prawns and potatoes – are found in most kitchens' emergency reserves. Frozen sweetcorn is preferable to canned sweetcorn, which has a salty, preserved taste. Serve with plenty of chunky, grainy bread.

Preparation time: 10 minutes **Cooking time:** 25 minutes

2 tablespoons olive oil

2 onions, chopped

2 celery sticks, sliced

1 litre (1¾ pints) chicken or fish stock

325 g (11 oz) potatoes, peeled and cut into small chunks

300 g (10 oz) frozen sweetcorn

150 g (5 oz) frozen prawns

1 tablespoon chopped thyme, coriander or parsley (optional)

salt and pepper

• Take care not to overcook the frozen prawns or they will be rubbery and tasteless. Prawns can be added to soups and stews while still frozen, then cooked gently until heated through.

Heat the olive oil in a saucepan. Add the onions and celery and fry gently for 5 minutes.

Add the stock and bring to the boil. Reduce the heat, add the potatoes and simmer gently, covered, for 8–10 minutes.

Add the sweetcorn and cook for 5 minutes, then add the prawns, and herbs, if using. Cook gently for a further 2–3 minutes until heated through. Season with salt and pepper to taste and ladle into warmed soup bowls.

BONUS POINTS
• Sweetcorn is a good source of complex carbohydrate and fibre, and contains protein, minerals, beta-carotene and vitamin C. It is beneficial for the nervous system and brain function, and may help to prevent certain forms of cancer.
• You can easily boost the vitamin content of this chowder by adding a green vegetable – such as broccoli florets, French beans or a sliced courgette – with the sweetcorn.

SALMON WITH PESTO & PASTA

Canned salmon might not taste as good as its fresh counterpart, but it's ideal for creating an easy meal in minutes. Bottled pesto sauce is another valuable storecupboard standby. For this recipe, use either the familiar green pesto made from basil and Parmesan, or red pesto – flavoured with peppers and tomatoes.

Preparation time: 10 minutes **Cooking time:** 15 minutes

325 g (11 oz) dried penne or other pasta shapes
2 tablespoons olive oil
1 onion, thinly sliced
400 g (13 oz) can red or pink salmon
150 g (5 oz) frozen peas
2 tablespoons pesto
1 tablespoon lemon juice
25 g (1 oz) Parmesan cheese, freshly grated
salt and pepper
Parmesan shavings, to garnish

Cook the pasta in plenty of lightly salted boiling water for about 8-10 minutes until almost tender.

Meanwhile, heat the oil in a frying pan, add the onion and fry for about 5 minutes until softened. Drain the salmon and discard any skin and bones. Roughly flake the flesh with a fork.

Add the peas to the pasta and cook for a further 3 minutes. Drain the pasta and peas, retaining a few tablespoonfuls of the cooking water, and return to the pan.

Stir in the pesto, lemon juice, Parmesan, onion and flaked salmon. Season lightly with salt and pepper and toss gently. Serve immediately, topped with Parmesan shavings and accompanied by a leafy salad, if liked.

BONUS POINT
• Some nutrients are lost during the canning process, but canned salmon is still a very good source of protein, essential fatty acids, minerals and vitamins A, B1 and D.

• Canned wild salmon is available from selected supermarkets. This generally has a superior flavour, but is slightly more expensive.
• For a milder flavour, substitute finely grated Cheddar for the Parmesan cheese.

BAKED POLENTA WITH CHEESE & TOMATOES

Many children like polenta, especially if they first taste it at an early age. As it is rather bland, polenta benefits from lots of additional flavourings, such as cheese, garlic and tomatoes. Serve with a fresh or frozen green vegetable, such as French beans, peas or broad beans.

Preparation time: 10 minutes **Cooking time:** 15 minutes

1 litre (1¾ pints) water

250 g (8 oz) instant polenta

50 g (2 oz) Parmesan cheese, freshly grated

2 tablespoons olive oil

1 onion, chopped

2 garlic cloves, crushed

400 g (13 oz) can chopped tomatoes

2 tablespoons tomato purée

4 anchovy fillets, halved lengthways

50 g (2 oz) Cheddar cheese, grated

salt and pepper

Bring the water to the boil in a medium saucepan with ½ teaspoon salt added. Add the polenta in a steady stream, whisking well so it doesn't become lumpy. Cook, stirring, over a moderate heat for about 5 minutes until very thick. Beat in 25 g (1 oz) of the Parmesan. Turn into a greased shallow heatproof dish and keep warm.

Heat the oil in a frying pan. Add the onion and garlic and fry gently for 3 minutes. Add the tomatoes, tomato purée and a little salt and pepper to taste. Bring to the boil, then spoon on top of the polenta.

Scatter with the anchovy fillets, then the remaining Parmesan and the Cheddar. Cook under a moderate grill for about 5 minutes until the cheese is melted and bubbling.

BONUS POINT
• Polenta provides energy in the form of starch carbohydrate, plus protein and minerals, such as iron and potassium. Polenta is a gluten-free grain and is therefore suitable for anyone with a gluten intolerance, but do check pack labels – some brands are coated with flour during processing.

• If some family members don't like anchovies, just scatter them over half of the dish.
• Other ingredients, such as chopped basil, olives and capers, can be used to flavour the sauce.
• Ready-grated cheese is a useful standby. When you have a spare moment, simply grate cheese into a tub or freezer bag, seal and store in the refrigerator or freezer.

SPAGHETTI CARBONARA

This recipe is a good choice when you're short of time and inspiration. Extra ingredients – such as halved cherry tomatoes or lightly cooked mushrooms, French beans, courgettes or baby spinach – can be added, depending on what you have in the refrigerator.

Preparation time: 5 minutes **Cooking time:** 10 minutes

300 g (10 oz) dried spaghetti

1 tablespoon olive oil

6 rashers of streaky bacon, thinly sliced

4 eggs

50 g (2 oz) Parmesan or Cheddar
    cheese, grated

salt and pepper

• For a better nutritional balance, increase the vitamins and fibre by adding an extra vegetable such as steamed mangetout, French beans or asparagus. Alternatively, serve accompanied by a leafy salad.

Add the spaghetti to a large saucepan of lightly salted boiling water and cook for about 10 minutes until just tender.

Meanwhile, heat the oil in a frying pan, add the bacon and fry gently until golden. Beat the eggs in a bowl with half of the cheese and season with a little salt and pepper.

Drain the spaghetti, retaining a few tablespoonfuls of the water, and return to the saucepan. Immediately tip in the egg mixture and bacon and toss the ingredients together until the egg starts to set. The heat of the pasta alone is usually sufficient to lightly cook the egg. If it is still very runny after a minute or two, toss over a low heat briefly.

Transfer to serving plates, sprinkle with the remaining cheese and serve.

BONUS POINTS
• Eggs are an excellent source of protein. They also supply vitamins A, B12 and D, plus a variety of important minerals.
• As the eggs are well disguised in this recipe, it's a good one to give children who aren't keen on this valuable food in its usual cooked forms.

FRENCH BEAN & CHORIZO OMELETTE

Spicy, garlicky chorizo sausage is great for enlivening all kinds of dishes, from soups and stews to pilafs and pasta. Here it adds colour and bite to a simple omelette. Serve with some warm, crusty bread and a simple tomato and olive salad for an effortless light lunch or supper. **Serves 2**

Preparation time: 5 minutes **Cooking time:** 10 minutes

150 g (5 oz) frozen French beans

1 tablespoon olive oil

15 g (½ oz) butter

1 red onion, chopped

4 eggs, beaten

25 g (1 oz) chorizo sausage, thinly sliced

50 g (2 oz) Cheddar cheese, grated

salt and pepper

• You will need to use a frying pan that is suitable for placing under the grill.

Add the French beans to a saucepan of lightly salted boiling water and cook for 2 minutes, then drain.

Heat the oil and butter in a medium frying pan. Add the onion and fry gently for 3 minutes until softened. Add the eggs and season with salt and pepper. Cook gently for 2–3 minutes until they are lightly set, pushing the cooked edges of the omelette towards the centre so the uncooked mixture fills the pan.

Scatter the beans and chorizo over the surface of the omelette and then sprinkle with the cheese. Place under a preheated moderate grill for about 2 minutes until the cheese has melted.

BONUS POINTS

• Like meat, fish and dairy produce, eggs contain all of the essential amino acids that are vital for a healthy diet.

• Onions are a rather underrated vegetable in nutritional terms. They provide various nutrients including calcium, magnesium, beta-carotene and folic acid.

CHILLI BEAN BAKE

A wonderful, comforting pie with a layered potato topping under a crust of melting cheese. You can serve it as a complete meal on its own, or accompanied by lightly cooked French beans, steamed broccoli or a spinach, watercress or mixed leaf salad.

Preparation time: 15 minutes **Cooking time:** 50 minutes

3 tablespoons olive oil

1 onion, chopped

2 garlic cloves, crushed

150 g (5 oz) chestnut mushrooms, halved

2 teaspoons mild chilli powder

400 g (13 oz) can red kidney beans, rinsed and drained

250 ml (8 fl oz) carrot juice

2 tablespoons tomato purée

750 g (1½ lb) new potatoes

50 g (2 oz) Gruyère or Cheddar cheese, grated

salt and pepper

Heat the oil in a saucepan, add the onion and garlic and fry gently for about 5 minutes. Add the mushrooms and fry for 2 minutes.

Stir in the chilli powder, kidney beans, carrot juice, tomato purée and a little salt and pepper. Bring to the boil, then lower the heat, cover and simmer gently for 5 minutes. Turn into a 1.8 litre (3 pint) ovenproof dish.

Scrub the potatoes and slice them thinly. Cook in lightly salted boiling water for 5 minutes; drain thoroughly.

Layer the potatoes over the bean mixture and scatter the cheese on top. Bake in a preheated oven at 200°C (400°F) Gas Mark 6 for about 30 minutes until the surface is golden.

BONUS POINT
• Red kidney beans are a useful source of potassium, magnesium, zinc, protein and folic acid. Folic acid is essential for brain and nerve function, and for utilizing protein.

• This makes a good freeze-ahead dish for vegetarian members of the family. Cook it in individual pie dishes or disposable foil dishes and freeze for up to 3 months.
• A carton or can of carrot juice makes a good storecupboard standby. It can be used instead of stock in flavoursome sauces for vegetable dishes.

74

CHICKPEA & POTATO CURRY

A good midweek recipe when you fancy something spicy, healthy and fast! The juice from the tomatoes reduces and thickens as it cooks to give an intensely flavoured sauce. Serve the curry with basmati rice, naan or plenty of grainy bread, plus your favourite chutney and a salad.

Preparation time: 5 minutes **Cooking time:** 25 minutes

2 tablespoons sunflower or other
    vegetable oil
1 large onion, chopped
1 teaspoon ground turmeric
2 teaspoons medium curry paste
1 large baking potato, diced
400 g (13 oz) can chickpeas, rinsed and
    drained
800 g (1 lb 10 oz) can plum tomatoes
2 teaspoons muscovado sugar
small handful of coriander, chopped
salt and pepper

Heat the oil in a large saucepan. Add the onion, turmeric, curry paste and diced potato and fry gently for 5 minutes.

Add the chickpeas, tomatoes, sugar and a little salt and pepper. Bring to the boil, then reduce the heat and cook, uncovered, for about 20 minutes until pulpy, stirring frequently and breaking up the tomatoes.

Stir in the chopped coriander and check the seasoning. Serve with basmati rice or bread.

BONUS POINT
• Chickpeas contain useful amounts of protein, fibre, magnesium and iron. Both chickpeas and potatoes provide slow-release carbohydrate that helps keep energy levels high.

• Canned beans, such as pinto, borlotti or red kidney beans, can be used instead of chickpeas. Add them halfway through cooking as they're more inclined to break up than chickpeas.

BLUE CHEESE & BROCCOLI RISOTTO

Deliciously creamy, versatile and easy to eat, risotto is an ideal family meal. You can use it as a base for a wealth of different flavours – here broccoli and blue cheese are a sublime combination. Together with the rice, they provide a highly nutritious lunch or supper dish.

Preparation time: 15 minutes **Cooking time:** about 30 minutes

200 g (7 oz) fresh or frozen broccoli

25 g (1 oz) butter

1 tablespoon olive oil

400 g (13 oz) risotto rice

2 garlic cloves, crushed

1.2 litres (2 pints) hot chicken or vegetable stock

125 g (4 oz) dolcelatte, Gorgonzola or other blue cheese, crumbled

salt and pepper

• Traditionally, risottos are made by gradually adding the stock to the pan and stirring continuously to achieve the perfect consistency. This time-saving version produces very acceptable results.

• Other green vegetables – such as asparagus, peas, mangetout, French beans or broad beans – can be used instead of the broccoli.

If you are using fresh broccoli, break it into florets and thinly slice the stalks. Steam fresh or frozen broccoli for 5 minutes, or cook it in a little boiling water until just tender.

Meanwhile, melt the butter with the oil in a large, heavy-based saucepan. Add the rice and garlic and cook, stirring, for 1 minute. Add about 150 ml (¼ pint) of the hot stock and stir until the stock is almost totally absorbed.

Add the remaining stock and bring to the boil. Reduce the heat and cook, uncovered, for about 20–25 minutes until the rice is tender and the risotto is pulpy. Stir several times during cooking and add a little boiling water if the mixture becomes dry.

Add the broccoli, cheese and salt and pepper to taste. Stir gently over a low heat for 1 minute. Serve immediately.

BONUS POINTS

• Steaming vegetables takes a little longer than boiling them but nutrients that would otherwise be lost in the cooking water are retained. If you don't have a steaming pan, a small expandable metal steamer is a worthwhile investment as it can be fitted into most average saucepans with lids.

• Broccoli is an excellent source of vitamin C, as well as potassium. Like cauliflower and cabbage it has cancer-inhibiting properties.

BEAN & TOMATO COUSCOUS

This recipe includes the classic couscous ingredients, minus the meat! Plenty of vegetables, beans, spices and dried fruit provide ample flavour and create an appetizing dish that's equally suitable for lunch or supper. There's plenty of scope for variations, too. You can include any odd fresh vegetables that you happen to have in the refrigerator – such as red peppers, courgettes, mushrooms or French beans.

Preparation time: 10 minutes **Cooking time:** 25 minutes

3 tablespoons olive oil

1 large onion, chopped

2 celery sticks, sliced

2 garlic cloves, crushed

400 g (13 oz) can chopped tomatoes

1 teaspoon ground cumin

1 teaspoon ground coriander

1 tablespoon paprika

400 g (13 oz) can mixed beans, cannellini or haricot beans, rinsed and drained

400 g (13 oz) can chickpeas, rinsed and drained

50 g (2 oz) dried apricots, sliced

300 ml (½ pint) chicken or vegetable stock

250 g (8 oz) couscous

salt and pepper

celery leaves (if available), to garnish

Heat the oil in a large saucepan. Add the onion, celery and garlic and fry gently for 5 minutes.

Stir in the tomatoes, spices, beans, chickpeas, dried apricots and stock and bring to the boil. Reduce the heat and simmer gently, uncovered, for about 20 minutes until the vegetables are tender and the sauce is pulpy.

Meanwhile, put the couscous into a bowl with a little salt and pepper. Add 300 ml (½ pint) boiling water and cover with foil. Leave in a warm place for 5–10 minutes until the water has been absorbed. Fluff up lightly with a fork.

Spoon the couscous on to warmed serving plates and top with the sauce. Garnish with celery leaves, if available.

BONUS POINTS
• Chickpeas are an excellent source of vegetable protein, slow-release carbohydrate and fibre. They help to steady blood sugar levels and cleanse the digestive system.
• Provided vegetable stock is used, this recipe is suitable for vegans.

• If you are including extra fresh vegetables in the couscous, chop them roughly and add them with the chickpeas. Add frozen beans or peas towards the end of cooking.

Kids' Teas

It's so tempting to reach for a can of baked beans or spaghetti for small children's teas, especially if they've eaten a good lunch and you have a later meal to cook for the rest of the family. These recipes are specifically designed to appeal to young tastebuds, and are prepared in minutes – using everyday, nutritious ingredients. In some cases, leftovers can be chilled for lunch or tea the next day.

PIZZA QUICHES

Thinly rolled puff pastry makes a quick, easy alternative pizza base, conveniently rising up around the filling to encase it. Filled with pepperoni, cherry tomatoes and cheese, these are somewhere between a mini quiche and a pizza. They are delicious served warm or cold. **Makes 6**

Preparation time: 10 minutes **Cooking time:** 20 minutes

500 g (1 lb) puff pastry
3 tablespoons sun-dried tomato paste
375 g (12 oz) cherry tomatoes, halved
50 g (2 oz) pepperoni, thinly sliced
125 g (4 oz) mozzarella cheese, thinly
    sliced
1 tablespoon olive oil

Lightly oil a large baking sheet and sprinkle with a little water. Thinly roll out the pastry on a lightly floured surface and cut out six 10 cm (4 inch) rounds, using a saucer as a guide. Transfer to the prepared baking sheet.

Spread with the tomato paste, to within 1 cm (½ inch) of the edges. Pile the cherry tomatoes, pepperoni and mozzarella on top.

Drizzle with the oil and bake in a preheated oven at 200°C (400°F) Gas Mark 6 for 20 minutes until the pastry is well risen and golden, and the cheese has melted. Serve warm.

BONUS POINTS
• Fresh tomatoes are rich in the antioxidant lycopene that helps protect cells from damage, including some forms of cancer. The fat in the cheese helps the body absorb lycopene.
• Serve these pizza quiches with salad vegetables, such as carrot, cucumber and celery sticks, to add fibre, plus extra vitamins and minerals.

• Vary the topping to suit individual tastes – sliced peppers, cooked chicken and pineapple are popular with children.

BABY JACKETS WITH SARDINES

Small roast potatoes cook quickly and are less of a marathon for children to eat than large baking potatoes. Remember to pop the potatoes into the oven well in advance and you couldn't have an easier meal. Serve with broccoli, French beans or a simple salad. **Serves 2**

Preparation time: 5 minutes **Cooking time:** 40 minutes

4 small potatoes, about 300 g (10 oz)

2 teaspoons olive oil

100 g (3½ oz) can sardines in tomato sauce

1 tablespoon mayonnaise

3 tablespoons Greek yogurt

• Pilchards, a larger member of the sardine family, or canned tuna can be used instead of sardines.

• Use any leftover topping for filling sandwiches or serving as a dip with vegetable sticks the next day.

Halve the potatoes lengthways. Place, cut-side up, in a small ovenproof dish and brush with the oil. Bake in a preheated oven at 200°C (400°F) Gas Mark 6 for about 40 minutes until tender and golden.

Mash the sardines in a bowl to break them into small pieces and fold in the mayonnaise and yogurt. Spoon on to the potato halves to serve.

BONUS POINTS
• Sardines are rich in vitamins, minerals and the essential omega-3 fatty acids. The canning process softens the calcium-rich bones, so you can simply mash them with the sardine flesh.
• Whole potatoes, baked in their skins, retain more nutrients than peeled boiled potatoes.

VEGGIE CHIPS WITH TUNA DIP

Homemade oven chips, cut from potatoes, carrots and parsnips, taste far superior to ready-made frozen ones and provide more nutrients – with little extra effort. It's worth making a double quantity of dip, so you have some left for topping jacket potatoes, or filling pittas and sandwiches. **Serves 2**

Preparation time: 10 minutes **Cooking time:** 45 minutes

375 g (12 oz) potatoes, scrubbed

2 large carrots, halved

2 parsnips, halved

2 tablespoons vegetable oil

100 g (3½ oz) can tuna in brine

1 tablespoon mayonnaise

1 tablespoon natural yogurt

1 teaspoon tomato purée

paprika, for sprinkling (optional)

Cut the potatoes, carrots and parsnips lengthways into similar-sized chunky wedges. Cook in a pan of boiling water for 5 minutes to partially soften.

Drain the vegetables thoroughly and transfer to a roasting tin. Add the oil and toss gently. Bake in a preheated oven at 200°C (400°F) Gas Mark 6 for about 40 minutes until crisp and golden.

Meanwhile, drain the tuna and put it in a bowl with the mayonnaise, yogurt and tomato purée. Beat to blend thoroughly. Turn into two small bowls and place on serving plates.

Surround the bowls of dip with the veggie chips and sprinkle with paprika to serve if liked.

BONUS POINT
• Root vegetables are an excellent source of slow-release carbohydrate, that provide us with sustained energy. Other good sources include dark green vegetables, fruit, wholegrains, beans and pulses.

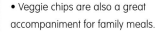

• Veggie chips are also a great accompaniment for family meals.

GRIDDLED TUNA MUFFINS

Far more exciting than a regular sandwich, these toasted split muffins are deep-filled with a tangy tuna salad to make a meal in themselves, rather like a burger. If you do not have a griddle pan, lightly toast the muffins under the grill. **Serves 2**

Preparation time: 5 minutes **Cooking time:** 4 minutes

100 g (3½ oz) can tuna in brine, drained
2 tablespoons tomato ketchup
4 teaspoons balsamic or wine vinegar
2 wholemeal or white muffins, split
small handful of fresh baby spinach
    leaves, about 25 g (1 oz)
2 small tomatoes, thinly sliced
a little oil, for cooking

• For extra zest, add gherkin slices or chopped fresh herbs to the filling.
• One muffin is sufficient for a small child; an older child might eat two.

Put the tuna in a bowl and break it into small pieces with a fork.

Mix together the tomato ketchup and vinegar and spread over the cut surfaces of the muffins.

Pile the tuna on the muffin bases and scatter with the spinach. Add the tomato slices, then the muffin tops and press down firmly to make them more compact.

Lightly oil a griddle pan and cook the muffins gently on one side until toasted. Turn them over carefully and cook until the underside is toasted. Serve warm.

BONUS POINT
• Tuna canned in brine rather than oil contains about a quarter of the amount of fat. The resulting 'drier' texture can easily be overcome with a dressing such as the one used above, which gives it a lovely, moist, tangy flavour.

HASHED SWEET POTATOES WITH EGGS

Introducing children to slightly more unusual vegetables when they're young encourages them towards a varied – and more interesting – diet. Sweet potatoes have a distinctive, earthy sweetness that's lovely with peppers and onion. You could use half sweet and half ordinary potatoes to subtly introduce the new flavour, or all potatoes if preferred. **Serves 2**

Preparation time: 15 minutes **Cooking time:** 20 minutes

375 g (12 oz) sweet potatoes

3 tablespoons olive or vegetable oil

1 red onion, chopped

1 garlic clove, crushed (optional)

2 teaspoons paprika

1 red pepper, cored, deseeded and
    chopped

1 green pepper, cored, deseeded and
    chopped

2 eggs

Scrub the sweet potatoes and cut into 1 cm (½ inch) dice. Add to a pan of boiling water and cook for 5 minutes until softened. Drain thoroughly.

Heat the oil in a medium, heavy-based frying pan. Add the onion and sweet potato and fry gently for about 5 minutes until beginning to colour. Add the garlic, if using, paprika and peppers and fry for a further 5 minutes.

Once the vegetables are soft and pale golden, make two cavities in the mixture, each large enough to take an egg. Break an egg into each cavity and cook gently until set. Pop under a preheated moderate grill to finish cooking the eggs. Serve immediately.

BONUS POINT
• Sweet potatoes are a highly nutritious food and easy to digest. They are particularly rich in beta-carotene, the vegetable source of vitamin A that may inhibit certain cancers. Sweet potatoes also contain vitamins C and E, potassium and other minerals.

• Make sure you use a frying pan suitable for placing under the grill.
• For older children, double the quantities and use a larger frying pan. Serve with chunks of grainy bread.
• Sweet potatoes can be baked in their jackets in the same way as ordinary potatoes. Scrub the skins, pierce with a fork and brush with olive oil before baking.

FRENCH TOAST SANDWICHES

Resort to this simple recipe when you are short of time and the refrigerator is rather bare. It is easily adapted to a sweet version: once the bread is cooked, soften some sliced apple, pear or banana in the pan, sprinkle the French toasts lightly with sugar and sandwich together with the fruit.
Serves 2

Preparation time: 5 minutes **Cooking time:** 3 minutes

4 thick slices of wholemeal bread, from a
    small sandwich loaf
2 eggs
4 tablespoons semi-skimmed milk
2 tablespoons light olive oil
75 g (3 oz) cherry tomatoes, halved
50 g (2 oz) Cheddar cheese, finely grated

• If your children dislike wholemeal bread, encourage them to eat grainy bread, which contains more fibre than ordinary white bread.
• Tuck some ham or bacon in with the tomatoes to make a more substantial meal.
• These toasts tend to brown really quickly after a minute or so. Take care to avoid burning them.

Trim the crusts from the bread slices. In a bowl, lightly beat the eggs with the milk and tip into a large shallow dish. Lay the bread in the egg mixture, leave for a few moments, then turn the slices over and leave until the egg mixture has been absorbed.

Heat the oil in a large frying pan. Add the bread slices and fry gently for about 1 minute until golden on the underside. Turn the slices over and fry for a further minute. Drain.

Add the tomatoes to the pan and toss gently for about 30 seconds until heated through. Place two French toasts on each serving plate and scatter with the tomatoes. Top with the remaining French toasts and sprinkle with the cheese. Serve immediately.

BONUS POINTS
• A great way of 'hiding' nutritious eggs in food for a child who is faddy about eating them.
• To up the protein and iron content, beat in a couple of extra egg yolks.

QUICK & EASY CASSOULET

As canned baked beans contain added sugar and salt, they can be used as the basis for a quick and easy meal that won't need additional seasoning. Look for low-salt, low-sugar baked beans, and buy the leanest sausages available. **Serves 2–3**

Preparation time: 10 minutes **Cooking time:** 45 minutes

2 tablespoons olive oil

1 onion, sliced

6 chipolata sausages

3 chicken drumsticks, skinned

400 g (13 oz) can chopped tomatoes

400 g (13 oz) can baked beans

1 tablespoon tomato purée

1 red pepper, cored, deseeded and chopped

100 g (3½ oz) French beans, sliced, or broccoli florets

25 g (1 oz) fresh wholemeal or white breadcrumbs

Heat 1 tablespoon of the oil in a flameproof casserole dish, add the onion, sausages and chicken drumsticks and fry for 5 minutes until they are beginning to colour.

Add the tomatoes, baked beans and tomato purée and bring to the boil. Cover with a lid and cook in a preheated oven at 190°C (375°F) Gas Mark 5 for 20 minutes.

Remove the casserole from the oven and stir in the red pepper and beans or broccoli. Sprinkle with the breadcrumbs and drizzle with the remaining oil. Bake, uncovered, for a further 20 minutes until the breadcrumbs are turning crisp.

BONUS POINT
• Cooking green vegetables in a casserole ensures maximum retention of water-soluble vitamins.

• For a quicker version, substitute drumsticks with chopped chicken breast, and chop the sausages. Fry gently in the oil with the onion until cooked through. Add the remaining ingredients (except the topping) and bring to the boil. Apply the topping and bake for 20 minutes only.

CHINESE CHICKEN WRAPS

These are popular with children of all ages, especially those who have developed a taste for Chinese food. Tortillas are lightly spread with spicy hoisin sauce, then rolled around cooked chicken and shredded vegetables to resemble Chinese pancakes. **Serves 2**

Preparation time: 10 minutes **Cooking time:** 8 minutes

2 small chicken breasts
1 celery stick
4 spring onions
10 cm (4 inch) length of cucumber
1 carrot
4 tablespoons hoisin sauce
2 large wheat tortillas
2 tablespoons sesame seeds

Thinly slice the chicken breasts and place them on a lightly oiled, foil-lined grill rack. Cook under a moderate grill for 3–4 minutes on each side until they are cooked through.

Cut the celery, spring onions and cucumber into 5 cm (2 inch) lengths, then cut them lengthways into fine shreds. Grate the carrot.

Spread the hoisin sauce over the tortillas to within 2.5 cm (1 inch) of the edges. Arrange the chicken slices down the centre and sprinkle with the sesame seeds and prepared vegetables. Roll up the tortillas to enclose the filling and serve.

BONUS POINTS
• A great way of getting children to eat raw vegetables and benefit from their high nutritional value.
• Sesame seeds, like pumpkin and sunflower seeds, are very high in the essential fatty acids that the body cannot manufacture for itself.

• An ideal recipe for using up chicken from a roast. Roast pork and lamb are also suitable.
• Hoisin sauce, a sweet and sour soya bean sauce, is available in jars from the Chinese section of supermarkets.
• These filled tortillas are perfect picnic food. Wrap them in napkins for easy eating.

AVOCADO SALAD WITH CRISP CROUTONS

Few children are keen on salads, but this tasty mix of crispy bacon, creamy avocado chunks and crunchy croûtons is really tempting – even for young tastebuds. **Serves 2**

Preparation time: 10 minutes **Cooking time:** 5 minutes

½ Romaine lettuce, or a large handful of
    baby spinach leaves
5 cm (2 inch) length of cucumber, diced
4 rashers of lean bacon, rinded and
    thinly sliced
2 thick slices of wholemeal or grainy
    bread
small knob of butter
3 tablespoons olive oil
1 avocado
1 tablespoon lemon juice
1 teaspoon grainy mustard

• Use this recipe as a base for your children's favourite ingredients. Grated raw carrot, beetroot wedges, diced peppers, sweetcorn, sugarsnap peas, diced cheese, hard-boiled egg wedges and prawns can be included to suit individual tastes.
• This salad is a good lunchbox filler and is quick to prepare in the morning before school.

If using lettuce, tear any large leaves into smaller pieces if required. Put the lettuce or spinach and cucumber in a bowl.

Heat a small frying pan over a moderate heat, add the bacon and dry-fry until crisp and golden. Remove with a slotted spoon.

Cut the bread into small cubes, discarding the crusts if preferred. Add the butter and 1 tablespoon of the oil to the pan. Heat until sizzling, then add the bread cubes and fry, turning, for 1–2 minutes until golden.

Halve, stone and peel the avocado. Dice the flesh and add to the salad with the crispy bacon and croûtons.

Mix the remaining oil, lemon juice and mustard to make a dressing. Drizzle over the salad, toss the ingredients together and serve.

BONUS POINTS
• Although avocados are high in calories, they're packed with nutrients. An excellent source of vitamin E, they also contain useful amounts of vitamin C and B vitamins, including folic acid – needed for brain and nerve function, and for the formation of red blood cells. Avocados also provide protein and minerals, such as potassium.
• Children who don't like cooked spinach often find milder raw spinach more acceptable. It's great in salads and highly nutritious – providing beta-carotene to protect cells, plenty of vitamin C and a variety of minerals.

TOMATO, BROAD BEAN & PASTA SOUP

Canned tomatoes and tiny soup pasta are the main ingredients in this comforting, minestrone-style soup. Served topped with crumbled cheese, it is delicious accompanied by lightly toasted grainy bread. **Serves 2–3**

Preparation time: 5 minutes **Cooking time:** 15 minutes

1 tablespoon olive oil

1 onion, finely chopped

400 g (13 oz) can plum tomatoes

½ teaspoon unrefined caster sugar

300 ml (½ pint) vegetable or chicken stock

2 tablespoons tomato purée

50 g (2 oz) soup pasta or small pasta shapes

75 g (3 oz) fresh broad beans

40 g (1½ oz) Cheddar or Gruyère cheese, crumbled

salt and pepper

Heat the oil in a saucepan. Add the onion and fry gently for 3 minutes until softened. Add the tomatoes, sugar, stock and tomato purée and bring to the boil. Reduce the heat, cover and cook gently for 5 minutes. Add the soup pasta and cook, covered, for about 5 minutes until the pasta is tender.

Stir in the broad beans and season lightly with salt and pepper. Cook gently for about 2 minutes until the beans are tender. Ladle into soup bowls and serve sprinkled with the cheese.

BONUS POINT
• This tasty soup provides a generous portion of one of the recommended five daily helpings of fresh fruit and vegetables.

• Canned butter beans or haricot beans can be used in place of the broad beans. Alternatively you could substitute sliced French beans, runner beans or peas.

Transportable

If lunch is away from home, it's easy to fall into the routine of a snatched sandwich and a bag of crisps. A repetitive diet soon becomes boring and can trigger food intolerances. If children take sandwiches to school, vary the fillings and type of bread – include some fresh fruit, vegetable sticks or salad in the lunchbox, too. The following quick and easy fillers for lunchboxes and picnic hampers provide a healthy variety – in the form of dips, pies, salads, interesting sandwich fillings and breads.

PEPPER & CHEESE PUFFS

These little pies are equally suitable for picnics and lunchboxes. For older children and adults you might want to add some chopped olives, garlic, chilli sauce or anchovies to the filling. If so, score a distinguishing mark – perhaps initials – on the uncooked pasties to identify them. **Makes 8**

Preparation time: 15 minutes **Cooking time:** 20 minutes

500 g (1 lb) puff pastry

beaten egg, to glaze

250 g (8 oz) jar mixed peppers in olive oil

400 g (13 oz) can borlotti or cannellini beans, rinsed and drained

125 g (4 oz) mozzarella cheese, thinly sliced

50 g (2 oz) Parmesan cheese, freshly grated

salt and pepper

• Refrigerate for up to 3 days. Freeze some for future use; defrost in the refrigerator overnight.

• For a balanced lunchbox meal, pack a tomato and cucumber salad, some fruit and a little muffin.

Lightly grease a large baking sheet and sprinkle with water. Roll out the pastry thinly on a lightly floured surface to a 33 cm (13 inch) square. Cut into 4 squares, then halve each square to make 8 rectangles. Lightly brush the edges with beaten egg.

Divide the peppers among the rectangles, keeping them to one half of each rectangle and at least 1 cm (½ inch) in from the edges. Scatter the beans over the peppers, then top with the cheeses. Season lightly with salt and pepper.

Fold the other half of each pastry rectangle over the filling and press the edges together firmly to seal. Brush the tops with beaten egg and score lightly with a knife. Transfer to the baking sheet.

Bake in a preheated oven at 200°C (400°F) Gas Mark 6 for 20 minutes until risen and golden. Serve warm or cold.

BONUS POINT
• Beans provide an excellent source of slow-release carbohydrate.

CHEESE & OATMEAL ROLLS

These are the solution if you suddenly discover you've run out of ordinary bread for lunchboxes. They are also great for an impromptu picnic – quickly baked and taken warm, loosely wrapped in foil. **Makes 8**

Preparation time: 5 minutes **Cooking time:** 20 minutes

200 g (7 oz) self-raising white flour

2 teaspoons baking powder

125 g (4 oz) medium oatmeal

50 g (2 oz) mature Cheddar cheese, grated

2 teaspoons Dijon mustard

4 tablespoons olive oil

1 egg, lightly beaten

5–6 tablespoons milk

Sift the flour and baking powder into a bowl. Add the oatmeal and cheese and mix together.

Beat together the mustard, oil, egg and 5 tablespoons of the milk in another bowl, then add to the flour mixture. Mix to a fairly soft dough, using a round-bladed knife and adding a little extra milk if the dough feels dry.

Turn out on to a floured surface and shape into a round. Cut into 8 wedges and shape each piece into a ball.

Place the rolls on a lightly greased large baking sheet, spacing them slightly apart. Score the top of each one twice, with a sharp knife. Bake in a preheated oven at 200°C (400°F) Gas Mark 6 for about 20 minutes until risen and golden. Transfer to a wire rack to cool.

BONUS POINT
• Oatmeal is a good source of slow-release carbohydrate that provides sustained energy. It also contains plenty of minerals and B vitamins.

• For a quicker picnic alternative, make 2 long sausage shaped loaves and bake for an extra 5 minutes. Cut into slices to serve.

• Flavour the rolls for adult tastes. Tuck drained, chopped sun-dried tomatoes, chopped mozzarella, basil leaves or olives into the centre of each roll as you shape it.

• Provide lunchbox variety by treating the bread just like ordinary rolls. Split and fill with salad, ham, sliced tomatoes, cheese, egg mayonnaise or tuna.

SWEETCORN & BACON MUFFINS

These little savoury muffins – packed with sweetcorn and bacon – make a welcome change from a sandwich school lunch. Alternatively, take them on a picnic and serve with a selection of cold meats and a salad. Store in an airtight container in the refrigerator for up to 2 days, or make ahead and freeze. **Makes 12**

Preparation time: 10 minutes **Cooking time:** 15–20 minutes

200 g (7 oz) frozen sweetcorn

4 rashers of lean bacon, rinded and finely chopped

150 g (5 oz) cornmeal

150 g (5 oz) self-raising white flour

2 teaspoons baking powder

50 g (2 oz) mature Cheddar cheese, grated

4 spring onions, finely chopped

200 ml (7 fl oz) semi-skimmed milk

2 eggs

1 tablespoon grainy mustard

2 tablespoons light olive oil

• Try different flavourings, such as red onion or leek in place of spring onions; or mushrooms or peppers instead of bacon for a vegetarian version. A sprinkling of chopped thyme or parsley is a tasty addition.

• Pack into lunchboxes with some cherry tomatoes, cucumber and carrot sticks, a piece of cheese and fruit, such as seedless grapes, an apple, or a halved kiwi fruit.

Lightly oil a 12-section muffin tin. Cook the sweetcorn in boiling water for 2 minutes, then drain and rinse under cold running water.

Heat a small frying pan over a moderate heat, add the bacon and dry-fry for about 3 minutes, until turning crisp.

Put the cornmeal, flour, baking powder, grated cheese and spring onions in a mixing bowl. Add the fried bacon pieces.

Beat the milk, eggs, mustard and oil in another bowl until evenly blended. Add to the flour mixture and stir until combined. Divide among the muffin sections.

Bake in a preheated oven at 220°C (425°F) Gas Mark 7 for 15–20 minutes until just firm. Loosen the edges of the muffins with a palette knife and transfer to a wire rack to cool.

BONUS POINTS

• These muffins provide plenty of vitamins, minerals, protein and carbohydrate. For a lunchbox, include fruit to boost vitamin levels and increase the absorption of iron.

• Served with a drink of fruit juice and followed by a tub of bio yogurt, these muffins also make a healthy family breakfast. If you have time, warm them to serve, to bring out their flavour.

CHICKEN & BEAN PATE

This unusual pâté has a delicious flavour that appeals to adults and children alike. Use very fresh chicken so that you can store the pâté in the refrigerator for a couple of days and use as required. **Serves 6–8**

Preparation time: 10 minutes **Cooking time:** 10 minutes

2 boneless, skinless chicken breasts

1 tablespoon olive oil

125 g (4 oz) quark or other curd cheese

400 g (13 oz) can red kidney beans, rinsed and drained

3 tablespoons red pesto

2 tablespoons lemon juice

salt and pepper

Cut the chicken breasts in half horizontally. Line a grill rack with foil and brush with a little of the olive oil. Lay the chicken breasts on the foil and brush with the remaining oil. Cook under a preheated moderate grill for about 8–10 minutes, turning once, until the chicken is cooked through and pale golden. Leave to cool slightly.

Put the chicken in a food processor and process until finely chopped. Add the curd cheese, red kidney beans, pesto, lemon juice and a little salt and pepper. Blend to a fairly smooth paste.

Transfer to a small serving container, cover and refrigerate for up to 2 days. Serve with grainy bread, or pitta breads.

BONUS POINT

• Lean chicken meat is a great source of protein, B vitamins and some minerals. Children need protein for growth, while we all need this vital nutrient for the formation of new cells to replace worn out or damaged ones.

• For wholesome lunchbox fillers, spread the chicken pâté in mini pittas, adding some sliced tomato and cucumber.

• For picnics, take the pâté in a small tub and serve with some interesting grainy bread, baguette or little rolls. The pâté is also delicious with rye bread and savoury scones.

• If the pesto is too pronounced for your children, flavour with some tomato paste or ketchup instead.

BABY TORTILLAS

In their simplest form, tortillas are Spanish omelettes layered with plenty of potatoes and onions. They are perfect for lunchboxes, because they have a more intense flavour when eaten cold. Baked in sections of a muffin tray, these mini tortillas have plenty of child appeal. **Makes 12**

Preparation time: 15 minutes   **Cooking time:** 20 minutes

375 g (12 oz) baby potatoes
1 small onion, finely chopped
6 eggs
25 g (1 oz) Parmesan cheese, freshly
    grated
salt and pepper

Lightly oil a 12-section muffin tin, preferably a nonstick one. Scrub and thinly slice the potatoes. Cook in a saucepan of lightly salted boiling water for 3–4 minutes until just tender. Drain and tip into the sections of the muffin tray. Scatter with the chopped onion.

In a jug, beat the eggs with the cheese and a little salt and pepper. Pour over the potatoes, to almost fill the muffin sections. Bake in a preheated oven at 180°C (350°F) Gas Mark 4 for about 20 minutes until the eggs have just set. Loosen the edges of the tortillas with a palette knife and transfer to a plate. Leave to cool.

BONUS POINT
• Potatoes are essentially an energy food, but they also contribute fibre, potassium and vitamin C to the diet. Nutrients are concentrated just beneath the skin of potatoes, so it's always better to scrub rather than peel them.

• Additional flavourings, such as chopped sun-dried tomatoes, pine nuts or shredded Parma ham, can be sprinkled over the potatoes before adding the eggs.
• For a balanced meal, add some raw vegetables to the lunchbox, such as celery sticks, carrot sticks and cherry tomatoes.

FETA DIP WITH VEGETABLE DIPPERS

Feta cheese with its fresh, tangy flavour is perfect for dips as it blends easily with yogurt – without engaging the food processor. Served with crisp vegetable dippers and grainy bread, this tasty dip makes an appetizing light lunch or picnic food. Leftover dip can be spooned over jacket potatoes. For picnics, serve with other dips such as hummus and guacamole. **Serves 6**

Preparation time: 15 minutes

250 g (8 oz) Greek yogurt
5 tablespoons mayonnaise
3 spring onions, finely chopped
100 g (3½ oz) feta cheese
salt and pepper

To serve:
selection of 4–5 vegetable dippers, such
as red and yellow pepper strips,
radishes, cauliflower or broccoli
florets, sugarsnap peas, carrot,
cucumber and celery sticks

Mix the yogurt and mayonnaise together in a bowl with the spring onions.

Crumble the feta into the bowl and stir in gently. Season with pepper and a little salt if required.

Spoon the dip into a container and seal. The dip can be stored for up to 2 days in the refrigerator. Serve with the vegetable dippers.

BONUS POINTS
• Eating vegetables raw makes available those nutrients that would otherwise be destroyed by cooking. In addition, chewing raw vegetables stimulates the enzymes that are crucial for digestion.
• Presenting food in a grown-up way is a good ploy to persuade children to eat healthily.

• A healthy lunchbox recipe for children who are old enough to manage a dip without getting into a mess. Spoon about 2 heaped dessertspoons of dip into a small tub. Pack dippers into a separate container, and add a chunk of grainy bread, a roll or some breadsticks to the lunchbox.

COUSCOUS & BEAN SALAD

Couscous has such a gentle flavour and soft texture that it is usually acceptable to children of all ages. It's also very easy to prepare. Refrigerate any that you don't need straightaway for lunchboxes or the picnic hamper for up to 2 days and serve as an accompaniment to grilled chicken or fish together with a leafy salad. **Serves 6–8**

Preparation time: 10 minutes **Cooking time:** 2 minutes

250 g (8 oz) couscous
300 ml (½ pint) boiling water
100 g (3½ oz) French beans, trimmed
4 hard-boiled eggs, shelled
150 g (5 oz) cherry tomatoes, halved
400 g (13 oz) can red kidney beans,
    rinsed and drained
small handful of flat leaf parsley,
    chopped
4 tablespoons olive oil
2 tablespoons lemon juice
2 teaspoons hot chilli sauce (optional)
salt and pepper

• Pack the salad into small tubs for lunchboxes, remembering to include spoons.
• For fussy eaters, leave out the chilli sauce, parsley and even the dressing if necessary.
• This salad is also great for picnics as it can be prepared a day in advance, leaving the dressing to be added just before you leave.

Put the couscous in a large bowl, pour on the boiling water, cover and leave to stand for 10 minutes until the water has been absorbed.

Slice the French beans into bite-sized pieces and cook in boiling salted water for about 2 minutes, then drain and refresh under cold running water. Roughly chop the hard-boiled eggs.

Fluff up the couscous with a fork to separate the grains. Add the tomatoes, French beans, eggs, kidney beans and chopped parsley.

Beat together the oil, lemon juice, chilli sauce, if using, and a little salt and pepper. Add this dressing to the salad and toss the ingredients together lightly. Chill until ready to serve.

BONUS POINTS
• Couscous is a good carbohydrate food and an ideal 'carrier' for other nutritious ingredients such as vegetables, beans, chicken and fish.
• Bulgar wheat, another good quality carbohydrate, is a suitable alternative to couscous. Soak in boiling water in the same way.

MINTED PASTA SALAD

Pasta salads are great for lunchboxes as they provide a welcome change from the usual sandwiches and rolls. The addition of fragrant melon, ham, grated courgette and freshly chopped mint gives this salad a lovely fresh, summery flavour. **Serves 6–8**

Preparation time: 15 minutes **Cooking time:** 4 minutes

Cook the pasta in plenty of boiling water for about 3–4 minutes until just tender. Drain and rinse under cold running water.

Discard the seeds and skin from the melon, then cut the flesh into small dice. Mix the pasta, melon, ham and courgettes in a bowl.

Beat the honey, lemon juice, oil, mint and a little salt and pepper in a jug to make a dressing. Add to the salad and toss gently. Chill until required.

BONUS POINTS
• This nutritious salad provides a good balance of vitamins, protein and carbohydrate to sustain children through an afternoon at school.
• Orange-fleshed charentais melon is an excellent source of vitamin C and beta-carotene.

200 g (7 oz) soup pasta or small pasta
  shapes
½ Charentais or Ogen melon
100 g (3½ oz) sliced ham, roughly diced
250 g (8 oz) courgettes, coarsely grated
1 tablespoon clear honey
2 tablespoons lemon juice
3 tablespoons light olive oil
3 tablespoons chopped mint
salt and pepper

• This salad can be made in advance and kept in the refrigerator for up to 2 days.
• Halved seedless grapes, diced pear, apple slices or orange segments can be used instead of melon if preferred.
• For picnic food, you might prefer to use ordinary pasta shapes rather than tiny soup pasta.

ICED FAIRY CAKES

Little fairy cakes make easy lunchbox treats and most children love them, particularly if they're topped with glacé icing. They'll keep fresh for 3–4 days, and you can always freeze any that are unlikely to be eaten within this time.
Makes about 18

Preparation time: 15 minutes **Cooking time:** 20–25 minutes

125 g (4 oz) unsalted butter, softened

100 g (3½ oz) caster sugar (preferably unrefined)

2 eggs

75 g (3 oz) self-raising white flour

50 g (2 oz) self-raising wholemeal flour

½ teaspoon baking powder

75 g (3 oz) sultanas

finely grated rind of 1 lemon

75 g (3 oz) icing sugar (preferably unrefined)

1 tablespoon lemon juice

• Other dried fruit, such as chopped prunes, mango, papaya or pear, can be substituted for sultanas.

Line a 12-section and a 6-section bun tin with paper cake cases.

Put the butter, sugar and eggs in a bowl. Sift the flours and baking powder into the bowl, tipping in the grains left in the sieve. Beat with a hand-held electric whisk for about 2 minutes until creamy. Stir in the sultanas and lemon rind and spoon the mixture into the cake cases.

Bake in a preheated oven at 180°C (350°F) Gas Mark 4 for 20–25 minutes until risen and just firm. Transfer to a wire rack to cool.

Beat together the icing sugar and lemon juice until smooth and spread on top of the cakes. Allow to set, then store in an airtight container.

BONUS POINTS
• The natural sugar in the dried fruits enables you to cut down on the added sugar in these cakes.
• A proportion of wholemeal flour is used, rather than all white flour, to provide extra fibre, vitamins and minerals.

APPLE TEABREAD

This cake is fat-free and low in sugar, relying instead on plenty of dried fruit and apple juice to provide a sweet flavour and deliciously moist texture. It's made in minutes and can easily be knocked up on demand! Store in an airtight container in a cool place and it will stay fresh for lunchbox fillers right through the week. **Makes 10 slices**

Preparation time: 10 minutes **Cooking time:** 35–40 minutes

250 g (8 oz) mixed dried fruit
75 g (3 oz) light muscovado sugar
150 ml (¼ pint) apple juice
150 g (5 oz) self-raising white flour
½ teaspoon baking powder
1 teaspoon ground mixed spice
1 egg, lightly beaten

• For convenience, freeze individual teabread slices in small bags, transferring them to the refrigerator the evening before you need to pack them into lunchboxes.

Grease and line the base and long sides of a 500 g (1 lb) loaf tin with greaseproof paper. Put the dried fruit, sugar and apple juice in a saucepan and bring just to the boil. Remove from the heat, transfer to a mixing bowl and leave to cool for 10 minutes.

Sift the flour, baking powder and spice into the bowl. Add the egg and mix until evenly combined.

Turn into the prepared tin and level the surface. Bake in a preheated oven at 180°C (350°F) Gas Mark 4 for 35–40 minutes or until the cake is firm and a skewer inserted into the centre comes out clean. Leave in the tin for a few minutes, then transfer to a wire rack to cool.

BONUS POINT
• Dried fruit is a concentrated source of vitamins and minerals, such as iron – essential for healthy blood cells – and potassium – needed to help regulate blood pressure and for the transmission of nerve impulses.

Easy Entertaining

Busy lifestyles and family commitments call for a very relaxed style of entertaining, whether it's a special occasion, friends round for supper or a big family weekend lunch. The recipes in this chapter are quick and easy, nutritionally sound, but at the same time slightly special – entertaining needn't be all hard work! There are also suggestions for accommodating the tastes of young children should you need to do so.

SALMON CHERMOULA

6 skinless salmon steaks, cut from the
   thick end of the fillet

Chermoula:

2 teaspoons cumin seeds

1 teaspoon coriander seeds

¼ teaspoon crushed dried chillies, or
   1 teaspoon mild chilli seasoning

3 garlic cloves, crushed

finely grated rind and juice of 1 lime

3 tablespoons olive oil

15 g (½ oz) mixed coriander and flat leaf
   parsley, chopped

salt

• Omit the chermoula for younger children and cook their salmon in a separate dish, brushed with a little oil to keep it moist.

Chermoula, an aromatic herb and spice blend, is used here to envelop fish and impart an exotic flavour with little effort on your part! If you have time, coat the salmon in advance and leave to marinate, so it's all ready to cook. If not, simply prepare and cook in one go. Accompany the salmon with new potatoes, pasta or steamed couscous, and a tomato, avocado and red onion salad. **Serves 6**

Preparation time: 10 minutes **Cooking time:** 8 minutes

To make the chermoula, lightly pound the cumin and coriander seeds using a pestle and mortar (or a small bowl and the end of a rolling pin). Mix in a bowl with the chilli, garlic, lime rind and juice, oil, herbs and a little salt.

Put the salmon steaks in a shallow dish, add the chermoula and turn the fish to coat with the mixture.

Lightly butter a large, shallow grillproof dish. Lift the salmon steaks out of the marinade, reserving the juices, and lay them skinned-side up in the dish. Cook under a very hot grill for 4 minutes. Turn the salmon steaks and spoon on the remaining marinade. Grill for a further 4 minutes or until cooked through. Serve immediately.

BONUS POINT
• Salmon is rich in the omega-3 essential fatty acids that are vital for the brain and nervous system, immune system, heart and skin.

BACON-WRAPPED ROAST COD

This makes a great supper party dish or light weekend lunch – especially during the summer when a traditional roast is less appealing. Apart from the pesto dressing, the flavours are all fairly mild, so it should appeal to children too. Accompany with basmati rice or new potatoes, steamed sugarsnap peas or French beans, and some asparagus if available.
Serves 6

Preparation time: 20 minutes **Cooking time:** 25–30 minutes

150 g (5 oz) crème fraîche

4 teaspoons red or green pesto

750 g (1½ lb) skinless cod fillet, in 2 thick even-sized pieces

175 g (6 oz) courgettes, grated

1 small red onion, finely chopped

2 garlic cloves, crushed

small handful of basil leaves, roughly chopped

6 thin rindless rashers of streaky bacon

salt and pepper

basil leaves, to garnish

To make the dressing, mix the crème fraîche, pesto and a little salt and pepper in a bowl and set aside.

Pat the fish dry on kitchen paper and check for any remaining bones. Season the fish lightly on both sides with pepper and place one fish fillet in a small roasting tin.

In a bowl, mix the grated courgettes with the onion, garlic and basil and season with salt and pepper. Spoon the mixture on top of the fillet in the roasting tin, patting it down in an even layer. Place the second fish fillet on top with the thick end facing the opposite way.

Lay the bacon rashers over the fish tucking the ends underneath and leaving a little space between each rasher. Bake in a preheated oven at 200°C (400°F) Gas Mark 6 for 25–30 minutes until the fish is cooked through.

Serve the fish in thick slices with a little of the flavoured crème fraîche spooned over. Garnish with basil leaves.

BONUS POINT
• An easily digested meal, suitable for anyone on a low-fat diet.

• Buy thin streaky bacon rashers that are pliable enough to tuck under the fish neatly. If you can only get thick slices, stretch them by running the blade of a knife at an angle of 45° along each rasher.

• To check that the fish is cooked, pierce a thick end of a fillet with a knife; the flesh should flake easily.

MEDITERRANEAN ROAST CHICKEN

For a small party, it's quicker and easier to roast two small chickens rather than one large one – they often taste better too. In this version a garlicky paste is pushed under the skin so the flavours penetrate the meat, while the roasted vegetables save you having to think about accompaniments. However, if you do want to serve an extra green vegetable as an accompaniment, French beans or mangetout would go well. **Serves 6**

Preparation time: 20 minutes **Cooking time: about** 1 hour

3 garlic cloves, crushed

1 tablespoon chopped thyme or
    oregano

50 g (2 oz) cream cheese

1 tablespoon harissa paste

finely grated rind of 1 lemon

2 x 1.25 kg (2½ lb) oven-ready chickens

750 g (1½ lb) new potatoes

1 large aubergine, cut into 2.5 cm (1 inch)
    chunks

2 red peppers, cored, deseeded and cut
    into wedges

1 large fennel bulb, cut into wedges

3 large courgettes, cut into chunks

several thyme or oregano sprigs

5 tablespoons olive oil

salt and pepper

• Give younger children, who might not like the spicy stuffing, some of the leg meat or breast meat furthest away from the skin – it will have a milder flavour.

Beat together the garlic, chopped herbs, cream cheese, harissa paste, lemon rind and a little salt. Slide your fingers between the chicken breast and skin on both chickens to release the skin – try not to pull the skin away or tear it. Using a teaspoon, push the garlic mixture between the skin and breast meat. Smooth the skin back into place with the fingers so the paste forms an even layer under the skin.

Place the chickens side by side in a large roasting tin. Bake on the lower shelf of a preheated oven at 200°C (400°F) Gas Mark 6 for 20 minutes.

Meanwhile, par-cook the new potatoes in lightly salted boiling water for 5 minutes; drain. Put the potatoes in a separate large roasting tin with the aubergine, peppers, fennel, courgettes and herb sprigs. Drizzle with the oil and toss the vegetables to coat evenly. Place on the shelf above the chickens.

Continue to roast for a further 45 minutes or until the vegetables are ready and the chickens are cooked through. Check the chickens by piercing the thickest part of a thigh with a skewer; the juices should run clear.

Transfer the chickens and vegetables to warmed serving platters. Skim the fat from the roasting tin. Bubble up the roasting juices on the hob and serve with the chickens.

BONUS POINTS
• Chicken is an excellent source of protein for growth and repair of cells. It is also relatively low in fat (especially if you don't eat the skin).
• A variety of vegetables provides plenty of vitamins and minerals.

SPANISH CHICKEN WITH RICE & CHORIZO

This dish has a distinctly Spanish flavour though it is made with red rice, which comes from the Camargue in south-west France. Red rice is perfectly suited to oven baking because, unlike most types of white rice, it doesn't turn mushy if you leave it in the oven longer than planned – something that often happens when you're entertaining. **Serves 6**

Preparation time: 15 minutes **Cooking time:** 1 hour 10 minutes

2 tablespoons olive oil

6 chicken thighs, skinned

6 chicken drumsticks, skinned

1 large onion, chopped

2 celery sticks, sliced

75 g (3 oz) chorizo sausage

350 g (11½ oz) red rice

600 ml (1 pint) chicken stock

100 g (3½ oz) sun-dried tomatoes in oil, drained and sliced

50 g (2 oz) black olives

small handful of coriander, roughly chopped

salt and pepper

Heat the oil in a frying pan, add the chicken pieces and fry until lightly browned. Transfer to a large ovenproof casserole, using a slotted spoon.

Add the onion, celery and chorizo to the frying pan and fry for 3–4 minutes until beginning to colour. Add the rice and cook for 1 minute. Tip these ingredients over the chicken in the casserole.

Add the stock to the frying pan, bring to the boil, then pour over the chicken. Add the sun-dried tomatoes and a little salt and pepper.

Cover and cook in a preheated oven at 180°C (350°F) Gas Mark 4 for about 1 hour until the stock has been absorbed and the chicken is cooked through. Stir in the black olives and chopped coriander to serve.

BONUS POINT
• Red rice is much less refined than white rice and therefore provides more vitamins, minerals and fibre.

• The chorizo sold in most supermarkets is fairly mild with a lovely garlicky, paprika flavour that readily infuses all the other ingredients in this dish. Some delicatessens sell a hotter version – use this if you prefer a spicier dish.

CHICKEN & PARMA HAM WITH HERB DRESSING

Put together in minutes, this is the recipe to cook when you have friends over for lunch or supper and little time to prepare. Snatch a few moments to assemble the dish and leave it in the refrigerator, ready for cooking. Remember to bring it to room temperature before baking. Keep accompaniments simple – minted new potatoes and a dressed, leafy salad are all you need. **Serves 6**

Preparation time: 15 minutes **Cooking time:** 25–30 minutes

6 boneless, skinless chicken breasts

6 slices of Parma or Serrano ham

2 lemons

2 tablespoons capers, rinsed

2 tablespoons roughly chopped flat leaf parsley

2 tablespoons roughly chopped dill or tarragon

1 tablespoon olive oil

200 g (7 oz) Greek yogurt

salt and pepper

> • For children who aren't keen on the distinctive taste of Parma ham, use thin sliced mild-cured ham, and omit the capers and herbs.

Lay the chicken breasts between 2 sheets of greaseproof paper or clingfilm. Using a rolling pin, beat the chicken breasts to flatten them to about half their original thickness.

Season the chicken breasts on both sides with salt and pepper and place them in a lightly oiled large, shallow ovenproof dish or roasting tin. Scrunch up the Parma ham slices and arrange them over the chicken. Cut 12 lemon slices and put 2 slices on each portion. Scatter over the capers and a little of the chopped herbs. Drizzle with the olive oil.

Bake in a preheated oven at 200°C (400°F) Gas Mark 6 for 25–30 minutes until the chicken is cooked through. Test by piercing the thickest part of a portion with the tip of a knife; the juices should run clear.

Meanwhile, in a bowl, mix the yogurt with the remaining herbs and a little salt and pepper.

Transfer the chicken to warmed serving plates and spoon on a little of the sauce; hand the rest separately.

BONUS POINTS
• Yogurt is beneficial to the intestinal tract because it helps to regenerate normal 'good' bacteria in the gut. It is particularly useful for anyone who's been on antibiotics, which destroy some of these bacteria. If possible buy live bio yogurt, preferably organic.
• Yogurt is rich in calcium and vitamin D, and contains useful B vitamins.
• Skinless chicken breasts are low in fat and an excellent source of protein and B vitamins.

STIR-FRIED DUCK WITH BUCKWHEAT NOODLES

Stir-fries are great for entertaining because you can prepare everything in advance, including the sauce, ready for cooking at the last minute. Soba noodles have a lovely, nutty flavour and firm texture so they don't stick together, even if you slightly overcook them. You won't need any accompaniments, though you might like to follow with a leafy herb salad.

Preparation time: 15 minutes **Cooking time:** 10 minutes

4 small duck breast fillets

2 teaspoons cornflour

2 tablespoons rice vinegar

4 tablespoons hoisin sauce

2 tablespoons soy sauce

250 g (8 oz) dried soba noodles

2 tablespoons sunflower or vegetable oil

1 bunch of spring onions, trimmed and cut into 2.5 cm (1 inch) lengths

150 g (5 oz) shiitake or chestnut mushrooms, sliced

100 g (3½ oz) sugarsnap peas, halved lengthways

2 garlic cloves, sliced

5 cm (2 inch) piece fresh root ginger, grated

250 g (8 oz) can water chestnuts, drained and halved

Thinly slice the duck breasts and toss in the cornflour to coat.

In a small bowl, mix together the rice vinegar, hoisin sauce and soy sauce; set aside.

Cook the soba noodles in plenty of boiling water until just tender; about 5 minutes.

Meanwhile, heat the oil in a wok or large frying pan. Add the duck slices and stir-fry over a high heat until browned. Remove with a slotted spoon and set aside.

Add the spring onions, mushrooms, peas, garlic and ginger to the pan and stir-fry for 2 minutes until slightly softened, but still retaining texture.

Drain the cooked noodles and add to the vegetables with the water chestnuts and duck. Fry, stirring, for 2 minutes until heated through. Add the sauce and cook for a further 1 minute. Serve immediately.

BONUS POINTS
• Duck is rich in B vitamins, iron, zinc and selenium, an antioxidant mineral that aids the action of vitamin E and helps protect the body from viruses and certain forms of cancer.
• Because stir-frying is very quick, vegetables retain most of their heat-sensitive nutrients that are otherwise reduced by slower cooking methods.

• Soba noodles, made from a mixture of buckwheat and whole-wheat flour, are available from some supermarkets. They are highly nutritious and make a change from egg noodles or rice.

WARM THAI STEAK & NOODLE SALAD

Ginger, lemon grass, lime and chilli are flavours that typify Thai cooking. Here they add a delicious piquancy to grilled fillet steaks, which are served on a crisp, warm salad of vegetables and ribbon rice noodles. An ideal choice for summer entertaining. **Serves 6**

Preparation time: 20 minutes **Cooking time:** 10 minutes

5 cm (2 inch) piece fresh root ginger, grated

1 lemon grass stalk, thinly sliced

1 red chilli, deseeded and sliced

2 garlic cloves, crushed

5 tablespoons lime juice

1 tablespoon light muscovado sugar

2 tablespoons sesame oil

6 fillet steaks, each about 150 g (5 oz) and 2 cm (¾ inch) thick

250 g (8 oz) ribbon rice noodles

1 small head of Chinese leaves, shredded

100 g (3½ oz) bean sprouts

100 g (3½ oz) pak choi or spinach

salt and pepper

coriander sprigs, to garnish

• If you prefer your steaks well done, allow an extra 2 minutes each side under the grill.

• To keep last-minute preparation to the minimum, marinate the steaks several hours ahead and assemble the salad vegetables in a bowl, ready for heating through.

In a large bowl, mix together the ginger, lemon grass, chilli, garlic, lime juice, sugar and 1 tablespoon of the sesame oil. Add the steaks and turn to coat with the dressing. Leave for 10 minutes, or cover and refrigerate until needed if preparing in advance.

Cook the rice noodles in plenty of boiling water following packet directions until just tender. Drain and rinse under cold running water.

Lift the steaks on to a foil-lined grill rack. Spoon on the lemon grass and chilli shreds from the dressing, reserving the juices. Cook under a preheated very hot grill for 3 minutes on each side so the steaks are well browned on the outside but still rare in the centre.

Meanwhile, heat the remaining oil in a large saucepan or wok. Add the Chinese leaves, bean sprouts, pak choi or spinach, and cooked noodles. Toss together until evenly combined and warmed through. Add the reserved dressing and heat through for 30 seconds. Check the seasoning.

Transfer the noodles and vegetables to warmed serving plates and top with the grilled steaks. Garnish with coriander and serve immediately.

BONUS POINTS
• Bean sprouts are a good source of protein, B vitamins and vitamin C.
• Fillet steak is the leanest cut of beef. Combining it with lightly cooked vegetables makes this dish a healthy alternative to other red meat dishes.

GREMOLATA CRUSTED LAMB WITH TAGLIATELLE

Speedy, simple and made with relatively few ingredients, this recipe is perfect for dinner with friends or a special weekend lunch. If children are dining with you, cook their lamb without the crust if preferred, though the flavours aren't powerful and might be well received. **Serves 6**

Preparation time: 15 minutes **Cooking time:** 8 minutes

4 garlic cloves, crushed

finely grated rind of 2 lemons

small handful of flat leaf parsley, chopped

6 thick lamb leg steaks, each about 150 g (5 oz)

400 g (13 oz) fresh tagliatelle

375 g (12 oz) cherry tomatoes, halved

250 g (8 oz) mangetout, halved lengthways

6 tablespoons olive oil

4 tablespoons lemon juice

100 g (3½ oz) Parmesan cheese, freshly grated

salt and pepper

roughly chopped flat leaf parsley, to garnish

• Gremolata is a blend of garlic, parsley and lemon that can be sprinkled on to soups, stews, casseroles and pasta dishes. It imparts a delicious tangy, refreshing flavour.

Mix together the garlic, lemon rind, parsley and a little salt and pepper. Using a sharp knife, halve each lamb steak horizontally to make 2 thin slices. Place in a single layer on a lightly oiled rimmed baking sheet and press the gremolata mixture on top of the lamb to cover evenly. Grill under a preheated very hot grill for 6–8 minutes until cooked through.

Meanwhile, cook the pasta in plenty of lightly salted boiling water for about 3 minutes or until just tender.

Drain the pasta, return it to the pan and add the tomatoes, mangetout, olive oil, lemon juice and a little pepper. Toss the ingredients together until heated through. Stir in the Parmesan.

Pile the pasta mixture on to warmed serving plates and top with the grilled lamb. Scatter with parsley to serve.

BONUS POINTS
• Garlic is known as nature's own antibiotic! It has anti-bacterial, anti-viral and antiseptic properties. It's also a decongestant, helps to lower blood cholesterol and contains vitamin C, calcium and other minerals.
• The cherry tomatoes and mangetout are lightly cooked for maximum retention of nutrients.

EASY LAMB TAGINE

Spicy lamb and plump, dried apricots make a delicious combination in this simple version of a North African tagine. The chilli and coriander are added after the meat is cooked, so you can transfer child portions to a separate pan before adding these if preferred. **Serves 6**

Preparation time: 20 minutes **Cooking time:** 55 minutes

1 small butternut squash

750 g (1½ lb) lamb fillet

2 tablespoons plain flour

2 tablespoons olive oil

2 onions, chopped

3 celery sticks, sliced

3 garlic cloves, crushed

1 cinnamon stick, halved

450 ml (¾ pint) chicken or lamb stock

400 g (13 oz) can chickpeas, rinsed and drained

75 g (3 oz) ready-to-eat dried apricots, roughly chopped

2 teaspoons cumin seeds

1 red chilli, deseeded and finely chopped

4 tablespoons roughly chopped coriander

375 g (12 oz) couscous

350 ml (12 fl oz) boiling water

salt and pepper

Halve the squash and discard the seed pulp. Cut away the skin and cut the flesh into small chunks.

Cut the lamb into small chunks, discarding any excess fat. Mix the flour with a little salt and pepper and use to coat the lamb.

Heat the oil in a large saucepan or sauté pan. Fry the lamb in batches until browned; set aside. Add the onions, celery and garlic to the pan and fry for 3 minutes.

Return the meat to the pan. Add the cinnamon, stock, chickpeas, squash and apricots and bring just to the boil. Reduce the heat, cover and simmer gently for 30 minutes until the lamb is tender. Stir in the cumin seeds, chilli and coriander and cook for a further 15 minutes.

Meanwhile, put the couscous in a bowl with a little salt and pepper. Pour on the boiling water, cover with foil and leave in a warm place for 10 minutes.

Fluff up the couscous with a fork and divide between warmed serving plates. Add the lamb tagine and serve.

BONUS POINT
• Butternut squash is a good source of beta-carotene, the important antioxidant that is also used to make vitamin A in the body. Squash also provides vitamin C and important minerals.

• For convenience you can cook the tagine in a flameproof casserole in the oven. Once you have added all the ingredients (except the spices), cook at 170°C (325°F) Gas Mark 3 for 1 hour, adding the spices for the final 20 minutes.

ASPARAGUS & MUSHROOM LASAGNE

Smooth, creamy mascarpone may not rate highly as a healthy ingredient but it's an indulgence you can justify when it's combined with plenty of nutritious vegetables. It melts deliciously to make a simple creamy sauce.
Serves 6

Preparation time: 20 minutes **Cooking time:** 25 minutes

500 g (1 lb) asparagus
150 g (5 oz) mascarpone
1 teaspoon saffron threads
3 garlic cloves, crushed
3 tablespoons chopped fresh tarragon
4 tablespoons olive oil
12 sheets fresh lasagne
300 g (10 oz) mixed wild mushrooms or
    chestnut mushrooms, sliced if large
40 g (1½ oz) coarse breadcrumbs
salt and pepper

• This recipe is ideal to prepare and assemble ahead, ready to pop in the oven. Simply add an extra 5–10 minutes baking time if the dish has cooled.
• If you can't get hold of fresh lasagne, use dried sheets instead and adjust the cooking time.

Peel any tough, fibrous ends from the asparagus spears and cut the stalks in half. Lay the thicker stalk ends in a frying pan, cover with boiling water and cook for 1 minute. Add the asparagus tips and cook for a further minute. Drain and set aside.

Put the mascarpone in a bowl and crumble in the saffron. Add the garlic, tarragon and a little salt and pepper and blend until smooth.

Bring a large pan of water to the boil with 1 tablespoon oil added. Drop in the pasta sheets, one at a time, so they don't stick together. Cook until just tender, about 3 minutes. Drain and immerse in a bowl of cold water.

Heat 2 tablespoons of the oil in a frying pan and quickly fry the mushrooms until they are beginning to brown.

Drain the pasta and lay 6 sheets in a lightly greased large, shallow ovenproof dish, crumpling them slightly to fit. Reserve 12 asparagus tips and scatter the rest of the asparagus over the pasta. Dot with half of the mascarpone. Cover with another crumpled layer of lasagne and scatter with the mushrooms. Dot with the remaining mascarpone and place the reserved asparagus on top.

Sprinkle with the breadcrumbs and a little salt and pepper. Drizzle with the remaining olive oil. Bake in a preheated oven at 200°C (400°F) Gas Mark 6 for 15 minutes until heated through. Serve immediately.

BONUS POINT
• Asparagus contains vitamins C, K and beta-carotene. It's also a good source of folic acid, essential for brain and nerve functioning.

Desserts

Providing a homemade family pudding every day is neither practical for the time-constrained cook, nor desirable for maintaining a healthy diet. Fresh fruit and bio yogurt are the ideal way to round off midweek fast family meals. However, most of us love the treat of an occasional dessert and these mouth-watering recipes are quick, nutritious and irresistible.

POACHED APRICOTS WITH OATMEAL CREAM

This oatmeal cream is based on the Scottish Atholl Brose, comprising whipped cream flavoured with oats, honey and whisky. My lighter version of Greek yogurt flavoured with honey and toasted oats makes a delectable topping for poached apricots, peaches or other stone fruit.

Preparation time: 5 minutes **Cooking time:** 10 minutes

500 g (1 lb) fresh apricots

2 tablespoons light muscovado sugar

½ teaspoon ground ginger

75 ml (3 fl oz) water

40 g (1½ oz) medium or coarse oatmeal

200 g (7 oz) Greek yogurt

2 tablespoons double cream

2 tablespoons clear honey

Halve and quarter the apricots, discarding the stones. Heat the sugar, ginger and water in a saucepan until the sugar has dissolved.

Add the apricots and cover the pan. Simmer gently, stirring once, for about 10 minutes until just tender. Cool slightly, then spoon into 4 serving glasses or bowls.

Lightly toast the oatmeal in a dry frying pan over a medium heat for about 30 seconds, shaking the pan frequently; cool slightly.

Stir the toasted oatmeal into the yogurt, with the cream and honey. Spoon over the fruit and serve warm, or chill before serving if preferred.

BONUS POINTS
• Apricots are high in fibre, beta-carotene and potassium. They also provide vitamin C and calcium.
• Oatmeal is an excellent slow-release carbohydrate food, which provides sustained energy. It is also a good source of protein, fibre and B vitamins. The soluble fibre in oatmeal helps to lower blood cholesterol levels.

• Try using poached ripe peaches, nectarines, plums or greengages.
• Ready-to-eat dried apricots can be substituted for fresh ones. Use 250 g (8 oz); halve, then poach as above, using 200 ml (7 fl oz) water and only 1 tablespoon sugar.

QUICK & EASY SUMMER PUDDING

Unlike most summer puddings, this one doesn't need to be weighted down and refrigerated for several hours before serving. Simply assemble it before you prepare the main course, then pop it into in the refrigerator to chill.
Serves 6

Preparation time: 10 minutes **Cooking time:** 3 minutes

1 kg (2 lb) mixed summer fruits, such as strawberries, raspberries, redcurrants, blackcurrants, blackberries

100 g (3½ oz) caster sugar (preferably unrefined)

125 ml (4 fl oz) unsweetened cranberry juice

8 thin slices grainy bread, crusts removed

Halve the strawberries. Put all the fruits in a saucepan with the sugar and cranberry juice and heat gently until the sugar has dissolved and the juices start to run from the fruit.

Meanwhile, use about 6 bread slices to line the base and sides of a 1.2 litre (2 pint) pudding basin. Using a slotted spoon, spoon the fruits into the lined basin, pressing them down well. Cover with the remaining bread slices, cutting them to fit as necessary. Pour over the fruit juice remaining in the pan. Chill until ready to serve.

To serve, loosen the sides of the pudding with a knife and invert on to a serving plate. Serve cut into wedges.

BONUS POINTS
• Using grainy bread rather than white bread for this pudding raises the fibre and protein content.
• Soft fruits are very high in vitamin C, which is vital for healthy skin, bones and muscles. This important vitamin also boosts the immune system, helping to protect the body from viruses and other diseases.

• A little pouring cream or lightly whipped cream folded into an equal quantity of thick yogurt is the perfect accompaniment.
• Make this pudding when fresh soft fruits are plentiful and least expensive. Freeze for a special occasion, remembering to transfer the frozen pudding to the refrigerator the day before it is required.

MINI CHEESECAKES

These little baked cheesecakes are made with fromage frais and quark, which gives a light, mild flavour without the grainy texture of cottage cheese. The topping makes use of a good freezer standby – frozen mixed summer fruits, available in 500 g (1 lb) bags from most supermarkets.

Preparation time: 5 minutes **Cooking time:** 15 minutes

200 g (7 oz) fromage frais
250 g (8 oz) quark
1 teaspoon vanilla extract
40 g (1½ oz) caster sugar (preferably unrefined)
finely grated rind of 1 lemon
1 egg

Topping:
250 g (8 oz) frozen mixed summer fruits (raspberries, blackberries, redcurrants, cherries etc), thawed
3 tablespoons reduced-sugar strawberry or raspberry jam

Beat the fromage frais and quark in a bowl until smooth, then beat in the vanilla extract, sugar, lemon rind and egg until evenly combined.

Divide the mixture between 4 ramekin dishes. Bake in a preheated oven at 180°C (350°F) Gas Mark 4 for 15 minutes until softly set. Allow to cool.

To make the topping, drain the mixed fruits thoroughly, reserving 1 tablespoon juice. Melt the jam with the reserved juice in a small pan over a low heat. Arrange the fruits on top of the cheesecakes and brush with the melted jam to glaze.

BONUS POINTS
• Quark is a virtually fat-free soft cheese, made from fermented skimmed milk. It has a high protein level – about 12 g per 100 g (approximately 10%).
• Frozen fruits – like vegetables – are very fresh when they are commercially frozen. Consequently, they are sometimes more nutritious than their fresh equivalents that have been stored, first on a supermarket shelf and then at home. Lengthy storage results in some loss of vitamins – especially vitamin C.

• Thoroughly drain the fruits and dry on kitchen paper before using, or the juices will seep into the cheesecake bases.
• During the summer months when soft fruits are in season, top the cheesecakes with fresh sliced strawberries or raspberries.

GRILLED TROPICAL FRUITS

Fragrant, juicy tropical fruits make this speedy dessert rather special, but almost any fruits may be used. Passion fruit have a distinctive, exotic flavour that enhances any fruit salad, but they are not to everyone's taste – particularly children's – and can be left out if preferred.

Preparation time: 10 minutes **Cooking time:** 5 minutes

1 large mango
1 papaya
1 small pineapple
2 kiwi fruit
25 g (1 oz) unsalted butter, melted
1 piece preserved stem ginger, plus
   2 tablespoons syrup from the jar
2 passion fruit (optional)

• It's difficult to ascertain whether a mango is ripe when buying, as colour is not necessarily a good indication. Avoid blotchy fruits that have black spots, as these indicate over-ripeness. A ripe fruit should give very gently when pressed and have a slight fragrance.

Cut the mango lengthways, either side of the stone, then cut the flesh from the skin into chunky pieces. Halve the papaya, scoop out the seeds, then peel and cut the flesh into wedges. Cut the skin from the pineapple, then quarter it lengthways and cut out the core. Cut the pineapple flesh into smaller wedges. Peel and quarter the kiwi fruit.

Line a grill pan with foil, bringing the foil up over the sides of the pan to contain the juices. Arrange the fruits in the pan in a single layer. Brush with the butter and spoon over the ginger syrup.

Thinly slice the stem ginger, then cut each slice into thin slivers. Scatter over the fruits and grill for about 5 minutes until the fruits are beginning to colour. Transfer to serving bowls, adding any juices from the pan.

Halve the passion fruit, if using, scoop out the pulp and spoon over the warm fruit salad to serve.

BONUS POINT
• Mangoes are rich in vitamin C and beta-carotene, the important antioxidant that the body uses to make vitamin A.

BAKED APPLES WITH SYRUPY RAISINS

Although baked apples take a while in the oven, they're prepared in minutes and can be left to bake while you serve and enjoy the main course. A sprinkling of mixed spice or cinnamon can be added to the stuffing at your discretion – some children love spices, others don't! A dollop of Greek yogurt is the ideal complement for this dessert.

Preparation time: 10 minutes **Cooking time:** 35 minutes

4 large, sweet dessert apples

75 g (3 oz) raisins

finely grated rind and juice of 1 lemon

4 tablespoons clear honey

15 g (½ oz) unsalted butter

100 ml (3½ oz) apple juice

Greek yogurt, to serve

• Choose a naturally sweet, crisp apple such as Cox's or Braeburn, unless you prefer a tart flavour, in which case opt for Granny Smith's.

Using an apple corer, scoop out the cores from the apples, and peel if required. Place in a shallow ovenproof dish.

Mix together the raisins and lemon rind and pack tightly into the apple cavities. Mix the lemon juice with the honey and spoon over the apples. Top each one with a dot of butter and pour the apple juice into the dish.

Bake in a preheated oven at 200°C (400°F) Gas Mark 6 for about 35 minutes until the apples are tender. Transfer the apples to warmed serving plates and leave to cool for a minute or two. Tip the juices into a small pan and boil to reduce them slightly, then spoon over the apples. Serve with Greek yogurt.

BONUS POINT
• Apples contain vitamin C and some minerals. They are extremely high in pectin, a soluble fibre that helps to balance blood sugar levels and lower blood cholesterol levels. Soluble fibre also inhibits the absorption of undesirable heavy metals – such as cadmium, lead and mercury – traces of which are sometimes found in foods.

PLUM STRUDEL

For this mouth-watering pudding, ripe, juicy plums are wrapped in crisp layers of light filo pastry with a scattering of crisp, almondy breadcrumbs. Choose naturally sweet plums and you won't need much additional sugar.
Serves 4–6

Preparation time: 15 minutes **Cooking time:** 30 minutes

1 kg (2 lb) ripe plums (preferably Victoria)

25 g (1 oz) unsalted butter

50 g (2 oz) grainy breadcrumbs

½ teaspoon ground cinnamon

50 g (2 oz) ground almonds

75 g (3 oz) sultanas

50 g (2 oz) caster sugar (preferably unrefined)

3 sheets filo pastry, about 150 g (5 oz)

2 tablespoons sunflower oil

15 g (½ oz) flaked almonds

2 teaspoons icing sugar, for dusting

• Filo pastry sheets vary considerably in size. If you buy a pack of long, narrow ones, you may need to use extra sheets to make up the weight and arrange them in overlapping pairs to form a rectangle that's wide enough to roll.
• Try using other fruits instead of plums. Chopped dessert apples, pears, apricots and greengages are all suitable.

Halve, stone and slice the plums. Melt the butter in a frying pan, add the breadcrumbs and cinnamon and fry gently until crisp. Take off the heat and stir in the ground almonds, sultanas and sugar.

Lay one filo sheet on a clean surface and brush with a little oil. Cover with a second sheet and brush with oil. Cover with the final filo sheet and sprinkle with the crumb mixture to 2.5 cm (1 inch) from the edges.

Scatter the plums over the crumb mixture. Fold the two short ends inwards slightly over the filling then, starting from a long side, loosely roll up like a Swiss roll.

Place the roll join-side down on a rimmed baking sheet. Brush with a little more oil and scatter with the flaked almonds. Bake in a preheated oven at 200°C (400°F) Gas Mark 6 for about 30 minutes until golden. Leave to cool slightly, then dust with icing sugar and serve cut into slices.

BONUS POINTS
• Filo pastry is a lighter, lower fat alternative to other types of pastry.
• Plums contain vitamin E, an antioxidant that helps protect cells from damage, and may help to slow some of the effects of ageing.

PAN-FRIED ORANGES & BANANAS

Here the classic technique of frying bananas in a little butter is used to prepare a delicious, tangy dessert in minutes. Serve topped with spoonfuls of thick yogurt or scoops of good quality vanilla ice cream.

Preparation time: 5 minutes **Cooking time:** 5 minutes

2 oranges

25 g (1 oz) unsalted butter

1 cinnamon stick, halved

25 g (1 oz) light muscovado sugar

4 bananas, each cut diagonally
   into four pieces

5 tablespoons fresh orange juice

25 g (1 oz) broken walnuts, toasted

Using a sharp knife, cut the peel from the oranges, removing the white pith too. Thinly slice the oranges into rounds, discarding any pips; reserve the juice.

Melt the butter in a frying pan. Add the cinnamon stick and sugar and heat gently, stirring until the sugar has dissolved.

Add the bananas to the syrup and cook gently for 2 minutes, stirring frequently. Add the orange slices and juice and cook until the syrup is bubbling. Serve warm, scattered with toasted walnuts.

BONUS POINTS
• Bananas are an easily digested fruit and a good source of energy. They are rich in potassium, which helps regulate blood pressure and aids nerve and muscle function. Bananas are also high in fibre.
• Brief cooking helps to retain heat-sensitive vitamins, such as vitamin C.

• A good dessert to serve during the winter, when oranges tend to be at their sweetest and most juicy.
• This recipe lends itself to flavour variations. Try adding a handful of dried fruit, such as raisins or sliced prunes, apricots, pears or mango. Or use different spices like crushed cardamom pods, freshly grated nutmeg or allspice. Alternatively, stir in some thinly sliced pieces of preserved stem ginger in syrup.

RASPBERRY & PEACH MALLOW

Warming summer fruits in a light syrup really brings out their summery flavours. Here raspberries and peaches are enhanced in this way, then topped with a soft airy meringue, to make an easy, fast pudding for the whole family. Serve warm.

Preparation time: 10 minutes **Cooking time:** 8 minutes

2 ripe peaches, stoned and roughly
   chopped
1 tablespoon water
40 g (1½ oz) caster sugar (preferably
   unrefined), plus 1 tablespoon
250 g (8 oz) raspberries
2 egg whites
½ teaspoon vanilla extract
Greek yogurt (optional), to serve

• Other fruits can be used – such as ripe plums, gooseberries or greengages – or a combination of redcurrants and nectarines. You will probably need to add a little extra sugar for sharper fruits.

Halve, stone and roughly chop the peaches, then put them into a small saucepan with the water and 1 tablespoon of the sugar. Heat very gently until the peaches are slightly softened and juicy. Stir in the raspberries and then divide the fruits between 4 large ramekin dishes or small heatproof bowls.

Whisk the egg whites in a clean bowl until stiffly peaking, using a hand-held electric whisk. Gradually whisk in the sugar, a little at a time, until the mixture is glossy. Whisk in the vanilla extract.

Spoon the meringue over the fruits, spreading it to the edges of the dishes and piling it up in the centre. Lightly peak the meringue with the back of a spoon. Bake in a preheated oven at 210°C (425°F) Gas Mark 7 for about 5 minutes until the meringue is golden, keeping a close eye on the meringue as it will colour very quickly. Serve warm with Greek yogurt, if liked.

BONUS POINTS
• Meringue isn't considered to be a healthy food, but it is fat free and surprisingly low in calories. It's the whipped cream that's usually served with meringue that boosts calorie and fat intake. Here Greek yogurt is a healthier alternative to cream.
• Raspberries and peaches are both rich in vitamin C. Raspberries are also a useful source of vitamin E, folate and fibre.

APPLE FLAPJACK PUDDING

This simple recipe combines two favourites – apples and a crumbly, biscuity, flapjack topping. Serve warm or chilled, with a scoop of yogurt ice cream if you have some in the freezer, or a spoonful of Greek yogurt. Any leftovers can be popped into small containers for lunchboxes the following day.

Preparation time: 10 minutes **Cooking time:** 10 minutes

6 dessert apples

1 tablespoon lemon juice

2 tablespoons water

2 tablespoons clear honey

50 g (2 oz) dried blueberries or
    cranberries

25 g (1 oz) unsalted butter

75 g (3 oz) porridge oats

25 g (1 oz) ground almonds

3 tablespoons light muscovado sugar

• This simple crunchy topping is also good spooned over soft summer fruits, fruit salads, and chopped dried fruit and nut mixes.

• Sultanas or raisins can be used instead of dried blueberries or cranberries if you prefer.

Peel, quarter and core the apples, then halve each apple quarter. Put into a saucepan with the lemon juice and water and toss to mix.

Add the honey and dried fruit. Cover and cook gently, stirring frequently, for 8–10 minutes until softened and juicy.

Meanwhile, melt the butter in a frying pan. Add the oats and fry gently for 5 minutes until toasted. Add the ground almonds and sugar and cook for a further 2 minutes until toasted, golden and crisp.

Divide the apple mixture between 4 small serving glasses and sprinkle with the oat topping. Serve warm, or cool and chill until ready to serve.

BONUS POINTS
• Oats contain several important B vitamins, as well as minerals such as calcium that promote healthy bones and teeth.
• Apples contain plenty of pectin, a form of insoluble fibre that helps the digestive tract function smoothly.

PEAR & HAZELNUT PUDDING

This scrumptious pudding calls for ripe, juicy pears or, failing that, a large can of pear halves in fruit juice. For optimum enjoyment, serve topped with something creamy – but not too unhealthy – like Greek yogurt or a little pouring cream. **Serves 5–6**

Preparation time: 10 minutes **Cooking time:** 35 minutes

4 ripe pears
75 g (3 oz) unsalted butter, softened
75 g (3 oz) caster sugar (preferably unrefined)
25 g (1 oz) wholemeal plain flour
100 g (3½ oz) ground hazelnuts
½ teaspoon baking powder
2 eggs
1 teaspoon almond extract
1 tablespoon semi-skimmed milk
2 tablespoons roughly chopped hazelnuts
icing sugar, for dusting

• Most pears are sold firm and unripe in supermarkets. They need to be left at room temperature for 2 or 3 days to ripen before eating.
• Canned pears can be used as a substitute for fresh ones, but they need to be drained thoroughly.
• If you can't get ground hazelnuts, grind chopped hazelnuts in a food processor or blender, or use ground almonds instead.

Peel, halve and core the pears. Place the pear halves, cut sides up, in a shallow ovenproof dish so they fit in a single layer with a little space around them.

Put the butter, sugar, flour, ground hazelnuts, baking powder, eggs and almond extract in a bowl and beat with a hand-held electric whisk for 1–2 minutes until light and creamy. Stir in the milk.

Pour the mixture over and around the pears and scatter the chopped hazelnuts over the surface. Bake in a preheated oven at 180°C (350°F) Gas Mark 4 for about 35 minutes until golden and just firm to the touch. Serve dusted with icing sugar.

BONUS POINT
• Ground hazelnuts are a healthier alternative to white flour in this recipe. They are relatively high in fat, but this is in the form of unsaturated fatty acids (rather than unhealthy saturated fats). Hazelnuts are an excellent source of magnesium, which promotes healthy teeth and bones, and aids the functioning of muscles, nerves and metabolic enzymes.

Cakes & Bakes

These homemade cakes and biscuits are full of flavour and texture – a far cry from their refined, bought counterparts. Wholesome ingredients like porridge oats, oatmeal, wholemeal flour, nuts and seeds give texture, while the natural sweetness of fresh and dried fruits is used to excellent effect. By contrast, refined sugar provides all of the sweetness in most bought cakes and biscuits. In these recipes, fats are also reduced or dispensed with altogether. The results are delicious, fresh-tasting treats that can be relished by the whole family without wrecking the healthy diet.

APPLE SAUCE CAKE

125 g (4 oz) self-raising wholemeal flour
100 g (3½ oz) self-raising white flour
1 teaspoon baking powder
1 teaspoon ground cinnamon
75 g (3 oz) walnut pieces
75 g (3 oz) light muscovado sugar
2 dessert apples
175 g (6 oz) can sweetened apple sauce
3 eggs, lightly beaten
4 tablespoons semi-skimmed milk
1 tablespoon icing sugar, for dusting

• Nuts give the cake a good texture, but sultanas or raisins can be used instead.
• If preferred, make your own apple sauce: cook 2 chopped dessert apples with 6 tablespoons water and 2 tablespoons sugar in a small, heavy-based pan until tender, then purée until smooth. Add a little more water if the purée is very thick.

Tangy, easy-to-use, canned apple sauce gives this cake plenty of moisture and flavour, dispensing with the need for any butter or margarine. Delicious eaten on its own, this cake is also good served warm as a pudding, with a dollop of Greek yogurt. **Makes 16 squares**

Preparation time: 15 minutes **Cooking time:** 30 minutes

Grease and line a shallow 23 cm (9 inch) square baking tin with greaseproof paper or nonstick baking paper.

Sift the flours, baking powder and cinnamon into a bowl, tipping in the grains left in the sieve. Stir in the walnuts and sugar.

Peel, quarter, core and thinly slice the apples. Add three-quarters of them to the flour mixture.

In another bowl, beat the apple sauce with the eggs and milk until smooth. Stir into the dry ingredients and turn into the prepared tin.

Level the surface and scatter with the remaining apple slices. Bake in a preheated oven at 180°C (350°F) Gas Mark 4 for about 30 minutes until just firm. Leave to cool in the tin.

When cool, remove the cake from the tin, dust with icing sugar and cut into squares. Store in an airtight container in a cool place for up to 2–3 days.

BONUS POINTS
• This cake is relatively low in unhealthy saturated fats.
• Walnuts are a good source of B vitamins, vitamin E, and the essential fatty acids that are vital for healthy cells.

MALTY FRUIT CAKE

This cake is delicious on its own, or thinly spread with unsalted butter. The ginger adds a nice spicy bite but can be omitted if preferred. **Makes 10 slices**

Preparation time: 10 minutes **Cooking time:** 45 minutes

100 g (3½ oz) All-bran cereal
75 g (3 oz) dark muscovado sugar
150 g (5 oz) raisins or sultanas
350 ml (12 fl oz) semi-skimmed milk
2 pieces preserved stem ginger in syrup,
    drained and finely chopped
125 g (4 oz) self-raising wholemeal flour

Lightly grease a 1 kg (2 lb) loaf tin and line the base and long sides with greased greaseproof paper or nonstick baking paper.

Mix together the bran cereal, sugar, raisins or sultanas and milk in a bowl. Leave to stand for 10 minutes until the cereal has softened and the mixture is pulpy. Add the ginger.

Sift the flour over the ingredients, tipping in any grains left in the sieve. Fold the ingredients together, then turn into the prepared tin. Bake in a preheated oven at 180°C (350°F) Gas Mark 4 for about 45 minutes until just firm. Leave to cool in the tin.

When cool, remove the cake from the tin and store in an airtight container for up to 5 days. Serve cut into slices.

CHUNKY CHOC COOKIES

These delicious biscuits contain plenty of hidden goodness. They are best eaten within a couple of days of making. **Makes about 15**

Preparation time: 10 minutes **Cooking time:** 15 minutes

125 g (4 oz) porridge oats
75 g (3 oz) plain wholemeal flour
50 g (2 oz) plain white flour
3 tablespoons sesame seeds
3 tablespoons sunflower seeds
75 g (3 oz) unsalted butter
100 g (3½ oz) light muscovado sugar
4 tablespoons light olive oil
1 egg, lightly beaten
75 g (3 oz) plain or milk chocolate drops

Mix together the oats, flours, sesame and sunflower seeds in a bowl. Melt the butter with the sugar in a small saucepan. Add to the dry ingredients, with the oil and egg, and mix together until just combined. Stir in the chocolate drops.

Place dessertspoonfuls of the mixture on a lightly greased large baking sheet, spacing them slightly apart and pressing down with the back of the spoon to flatten. Bake in a preheated oven at 180°C (350°F) Gas Mark 4 for about 15 minutes until pale golden; the biscuits will still be slightly soft. Carefully transfer them to a wire rack, using a fish slice. They will firm up on cooling.

BONUS POINT
• Sunflower and sesame seeds provide protein, B vitamins and vitamin E.

CARROT & POPPY SEED CAKE

Fresh carrots give this delicious sponge cake a wonderfully moist texture, natural sweetness and plenty of goodness. A food processor, fitted with a fine grating disc, makes light work of grating the carrots. You can store this cake in an airtight container in the refrigerator for 2–3 days. **Makes 10 slices**

Preparation time: 15 minutes **Cooking time:** 40 minutes

250 g (8 oz) carrots

200 g (7 oz) self-raising wholemeal flour

1 teaspoon baking powder

1 teaspoon ground mixed spice

2 tablespoons poppy seeds

4 tablespoons molasses

125 g (4 oz) sultanas

2 eggs, lightly beaten

5 tablespoons light olive oil

6 tablespoons semi-skimmed milk

Topping:

125 g (4 oz) quark or other curd cheese

2–3 tablespoons icing sugar

Grease and line an 18 cm (7 inch) round cake tin with greaseproof paper or nonstick baking paper. Peel and finely grate the carrots.

Sift the flour, baking powder and spice into a bowl, tipping in the grains left in the sieve. Add the carrots, poppy seeds, molasses and sultanas and stir until combined.

In another bowl, lightly beat the eggs, oil and milk. Add to the carrot mixture and fold the ingredients together gently. Turn into the prepared tin and level the surface.

Bake the cake in a preheated oven at 170°C (325°F) Gas Mark 3 for about 40 minutes until it is just firm to the touch. Transfer to a wire rack to cool.

In a bowl, mix together the quark and icing sugar to make a smooth topping. Spread evenly over the cooled cake. Serve cut into slices.

BONUS POINT

• Molasses is a by-product of the sugar refining process and contains more nutrients – including iron and calcium than other sugars. However, like other sugars, it is quickly absorbed and only gives a short burst of energy.

• Quark – used for the topping – is a very low fat curd cheese.

• For convenience, bought ready-grated carrots can be used, as long as they are fine-textured.

• Substitute dark or light muscovado sugar if you cannot obtain molasses.

LEMONY POLENTA CAKE

Polenta and ground almonds take the place of flour in this easy cake, to provide a deliciously moist, nutty texture. Oil is used instead of butter or margarine, so there's no need for creaming or rubbing in – the whole lot is simply mixed together in one bowl. **Makes 8–10 squares**

Preparation time: 15 minutes **Cooking time:** 35 minutes

150 ml (¼ pint) light olive oil

175 g (6 oz) caster sugar (preferably unrefined)

125 g (4 oz) ground almonds

2 eggs

1 teaspoon vanilla extract

finely grated rind and juice of 4 lemons

175 g (6 oz) instant polenta

1 teaspoon baking powder

• If you do not have an 18 cm (7 inch) square tin, use a 20 cm (8 inch) round cake tin.
• Polenta, or coarsely ground cornmeal, is now widely available in supermarkets, in an 'instant' pre-cooked form. If you have semolina to hand, you can use it instead.

Grease and line an 18 cm (7 inch) square cake tin with greaseproof paper or nonstick baking paper.

Put the oil, 125 g (4 oz) of the sugar, the ground almonds, eggs and vanilla extract in a mixing bowl. Add the rind and juice of 2 lemons, the polenta and baking powder and beat well with a wooden spoon until the ingredients are evenly mixed.

Pour the mixture into the prepared tin. Bake in a preheated oven at 180°C (350°F) Gas Mark 4 for about 35 minutes until just firm to the touch.

Meanwhile, mix together the remaining sugar, lemon rind and juice. Remove the cake from the oven and immediately spoon the lemon sugar mixture over the surface. Leave to cool in the tin.

Cut the cake into squares. It can be stored in an airtight container for up to 4 days.

BONUS POINTS
• Lemons are very high in vitamin C, which is essential for a healthy immune system. Vitamin C helps to combat colds, coughs and sore throats.
• Olive oil is a healthier alternative to butter and margarine in cake recipes because it is high in beneficial monounsaturated fats, but low in potentially harmful saturated fats. The essential fatty acids in olive oil help protect body cells and facilitate the absorption of some nutrients.

BANANA & OAT SCONES

Baking bananas really brings out their flavour, which is used here to enhance plain scones. This quick and easy recipe is ideal for using up bananas that have sat a little too long in the fruit bowl. **Makes 9**

Preparation time: 15 minutes **Cooking time:** 10 minutes

125 g (4 oz) self-raising white flour

2 teaspoons baking powder

125 g (4 oz) medium oatmeal

50 g (2 oz) caster sugar (preferably unrefined)

finely grated rind of 1 lemon

2 small ripe bananas

4–5 tablespoons semi-skimmed milk, plus a little extra for glazing

porridge oats or extra oatmeal, for sprinkling

Sift the flour and baking powder into a bowl and stir in the oatmeal, sugar and lemon rind.

In another bowl, mash the bananas until broken into small pieces, but not to a smooth purée. Stir in the milk, then add to the dry ingredients. Mix to a dough, adding a little extra milk if the mixture is dry.

Turn on to a floured surface and gently pat out to a 20 cm (8 inch) square, about 2 cm (¾ inch) thick. Using a floured knife, cut the dough into 9 squares and transfer them to a lightly greased large baking sheet.

Brush with milk to glaze and sprinkle with porridge oats or oatmeal. Bake in a preheated oven at 220°C (425°F) Gas Mark 7 for about 10 minutes until well risen and golden. Transfer to a wire rack to cool. The scones can be stored in an airtight container for up to 2 days.

BONUS POINTS
• Banana and oatmeal are both high in slow-release carbohydrate, which provides long-lasting energy.
• Served warm, with yogurt and a portion of fresh or dried fruit, these scones make a nutritious breakfast.

• The secret of good scones is to keep the dough fairly soft and roll it thickly to make deep, moist scones – rather than ones that end up thin and biscuity.

• Try varying the flavourings: add a sprinkling of cinnamon or mixed spice; or a scattering of raisins or sultanas; or use grated orange rather than lemon rind.

• These scones are made more easily by cutting the dough into squares with a knife, but you can, of course, use a small cutter for traditional round scones.

COCONUT & BLUEBERRY CAKES

Moist, fruity and attractively dotted with blueberries, these little fairy cakes are perfect for teatime or as a lunchbox treat. They also freeze well so you can pop them in a freezer bag or container and take out individual cakes as required. Defrost at room temperature for an hour or so, or briefly pop in the microwave if serving at once. **Makes 12**

Preparation time: 10 minutes **Cooking time:** 20–25 minutes

125 g (4 oz) unsalted butter, softened

125 g (4 oz) light muscovado sugar

2 eggs

50 g (2 oz) self-raising white flour

50 g (2 oz) self-raising wholemeal flour

½ teaspoon baking powder

1 teaspoon vanilla extract

50 g (2 oz) desiccated coconut

150 g (5 oz) blueberries

• As an alternative to blueberries, use quartered fresh cherries, or dried blueberries or cranberries.

Line a 12-section muffin tin with paper muffin cases.

Put the butter, sugar and eggs in a mixing bowl. Sift the flours and baking powder into the bowl, tipping in the grains left in the sieve. Add the vanilla extract.

Beat with a hand-held electric whisk for 2 minutes until light and creamy. Stir in the coconut and blueberries and divide the mixture among the cases.

Bake in a preheated oven at 180°C (350°F) Gas Mark 4 for 20–25 minutes until risen and just firm. Transfer to a wire rack to cool. The cakes can be stored in an airtight container for up to 3–4 days.

BONUS POINTS

• Cakes made with half white and half wholemeal flour – like this one – contain more fibre than those made with 100% white flour, but they are not dry which is often the case when all wholemeal flour is used.

• Muscovado sugar is a natural unrefined raw cane sugar that has more flavour than refined white sugar. Light and dark muscovado sugars are widely available. Always buy these in preference to packs labelled simply 'light or dark brown sugar' which are usually refined white sugars with a little molasses added for colour.

ALMONDY FRUIT CAKE

This moreish, chunky traybake is packed with dried fruit and nut pieces. Fortunately it is low in fat and naturally sweet due to the high fruit content. **Makes 10–12 slices**

Preparation time: 15 minutes **Cooking time:** 30–35 minutes

250 g (8 oz) ready-to-eat dried apricots, roughly chopped

225 ml (7½ fl oz) water

75 g (3 oz) unsalted butter

150 g (5 oz) dried figs, roughly chopped

50 g (2 oz) sultanas

100 g (3½ oz) whole blanched almonds, roughly chopped

50 g (2 oz) dark muscovado sugar

1 tablespoon lemon juice

200 g (7 oz) self-raising wholemeal flour

2 teaspoons baking powder

1 teaspoon ground cinnamon

> • The fruit in this cake provides so much moisture that you can get away with using all wholemeal flour without making the cake dry. However, if preferred, you can use half wholemeal and half white flour.

Grease and line a 20 cm (8 inch) round shallow baking tin with greaseproof paper or non-stick baking paper.

Set aside 50 g (2 oz) of the apricots. Put the rest into a large saucepan with the water and bring to a simmer. Cover and cook gently for about 5 minutes until the apricots have plumped up. Let cool slightly, then tip into a food processor or blender and purée to make a thick sauce. Measure the volume and make up to 350 ml (12 fl oz) with water if necessary.

Return to the pan and stir in the butter until melted. Off the heat, add the remaining fruits, including the reserved apricots, nuts, sugar and lemon juice. Sift the flour, baking powder and cinnamon over the mixture, tipping in the grains left in the sieve. Gently fold the ingredients together.

Turn the mixture into the prepared tin and bake in a preheated oven at 190°C (375°F) Gas Mark 5 for about 25–30 minutes until just firm. Leave to cool in the tin. Serve cut into slices.

BONUS POINTS
• The apricot purée provides plenty of sweetness in this cake, so only a relatively small amount of added sugar is needed.
• Dried apricots are rich in beta-carotene, an important antioxidant that helps prevent cells from damage. Beta-carotene is also used in the body to make vitamin A.

REALLY FRUITY FLAPJACKS

Flapjacks are universally popular and they couldn't be quicker or easier to make. A generous mixture of dried fruit ensures that these flapjacks are naturally sweet – and packed with nutrients too. **Makes 15–20**

Preparation time: 10 minutes **Cooking time:** 20 minutes

75 g (3 oz) ready-to-eat dried prunes

75 g (3 oz) ready-to-eat dried apricots

100 g (3½ oz) unsalted butter

100 g (3½ oz) light muscovado sugar

5 tablespoons clear honey

375 g (12 oz) porridge oats

75 g (3 oz) raisins or sultanas

2 eggs

Lightly grease a 28 x 23 cm (11 x 9 inch) shallow baking tin, or a tin with similar dimensions. Chop the prunes and apricots into small pieces.

Melt the butter with the sugar and honey in a small saucepan. Remove from the heat and stir in the oats, prunes, apricots and raisins or sultanas until evenly mixed. Beat in the eggs.

Turn the mixture into the prepared tin and level the surface. Bake in a preheated oven at 180°C (350°F) Gas Mark 4 for 20 minutes until turning pale golden. Leave in the tin until almost cold, then cut into fingers and finish cooling on a wire rack.

The flapjacks can be stored in an airtight container in a cool place for up to 5 days.

BONUS POINTS
• This recipe contains about half the amount of sugar you would normally find in flapjacks, because the dried fruit provides sweetness.
• Eggs are an unusual ingredient in flapjacks, but they are used here to help bind the ingredients together in place of some of the sugar, and to add valuable extra nutrients.

• When you take them out of the oven, flapjacks are still soft in the centre. They firm up on cooling. Don't be tempted to cook them for longer or they will turn brittle.
• Other dried fruits, such as chopped figs or dates, can be used as alternatives to those listed above. For an extra tang, add the grated rind of 1 lemon with the melted butter.
• Make sure the fruit and oat mixture has cooled a little before you add the eggs or they will scramble in the heat.

CRANBERRY & OATMEAL MUFFINS

Dried cranberries add a lively tang and texture to these craggy-topped, muffins. Because they don't keep well, it's best to freeze any that won't be eaten on the day they are made. Simply remove them from the freezer as required, for snacks and lunchboxes. **Makes 12**

Preparation time: 10 minutes **Cooking time:** 15 minutes

100 g (3½ oz) self-raising white flour
100 g (3½ oz) wholemeal self-raising flour
1 teaspoon baking powder
1 teaspoon ground ginger
75 g (3 oz) medium oatmeal
125 g (4 oz) caster sugar (preferably unrefined)
75 g (3 oz) dried cranberries
4 tablespoons light olive oil
300 ml (½ pint) natural bio yogurt
2 eggs
extra oatmeal, for sprinkling

Line a 12-section muffin tin with paper muffin cases.

Sift the flours, baking powder and ginger into a bowl, tipping in the grains left in the sieve. Stir in the oatmeal, sugar and dried cranberries.

In another bowl, beat together the oil, yogurt and eggs until blended. Add to the dry ingredients and fold in, using a large metal spoon, until just incorporated, but with some dry grains still visible.

Divide the mixture between the paper muffin cases and sprinkle with a little extra oatmeal. Bake in a preheated oven at 200°C (400°F) Gas Mark 6 for about 15 minutes until just firm to the touch. Transfer to a wire rack to cool.

BONUS POINT
• Natural yogurt is a useful source of calcium, phosphorus, vitamin D and some B vitamins. It also contains natural bacteria that are beneficial to the digestive tract.

• Muffins are always at their best served freshly cooked, preferably with a little lingering warmth.
• If you can't buy dried cranberries, substitute dried blueberries, dried cherries, raisins or sultanas.

Index

Commissioning Editor:
Nicola Hill
Editor:
Tarda Davison-Aitkins
Executive Art Editor:
Leigh Jones
Production Controller:
Viv Cracknell

Project Manager and Editor:
Janet Illsley
Photographer:
David Jordan
Home Economist:
Sara Lewis
Assisted by
Celia Beard
Stylist:
Aruna Mathur
Designer:
Jo Tapper
Indexer:
Hilary Bird

Acknowledgements
The publisher would like to thank Ceramica Blue of 10 Blenheim Crescent London W11 1NN, for providing some of the crockery used in this book.